Easy Asian Cookbook

Easy Asian Cookbook

100+ Takeout Favorites Made Simple

KATHY FANG

Photography by Heidi's Bridge

ROCKRIDGE PRESS

Interior and Cover Designer: Patricia Fabricant
Art Producer: Sara Feinstein
Editor: Arturo Conde
Production Editor: Nora Milman

Photography © 2020 Heidi's Bridge. Food Styling by Sean Dooley.
Illustrations used under license from Creative Market.
Author photo courtesy of © Carolyn Shek.

ISBN: Print 978-1-64611-670-6 | eBook 978-1-64611-671-3

R0

I would like to dedicate this book
to my parents, Lily and Peter Fang.
I would not be where I am now if
it weren't for you. You lit the fire
that started my passion for food.
Almost every loving food memory
I have is associated with my parents,
and words can't express how blessed
I am to have experienced so
many with them.

CRAB RANGOON, PAGE 34

CONTENTS

❀

INTRODUCTION

❁

Food gives diners a sense of place and origin. Going out to eat at a restaurant serves more than one purpose. Aside from satisfying hunger, it provides an experience different from what you would get at home. When you dine at a Thai restaurant, for instance, you can taste flavors that are prevalent in Southeast Asia, such as sour, spicy, and sweet. You swap your usual steak and potatoes for sweet, aromatic coconut sticky rice; luxurious curries; and spicy rice noodles with crushed peanuts and bean sprouts. The servers may be dressed in traditional Thai apparel and there may be colorful prints and artwork on the walls, representing Southeast Asian culture and life. For a few short hours, you can imagine being transported to another country, eating as the locals do there. And if Thai doesn't fit one's fancy, then maybe Chinese, Japanese, Vietnamese, Korean, or another Asian cuisine will. This is the beauty of having access to so many different foods here in the United States.

The Asian immigrants who traveled to the United States seeking better opportunities brought with them their culture and food. In order to keep a part of their past alive and close to their hearts, they found ways to cook their own food using the resources and ingredients they could find in America. For Chinese immigrants, this meant cooking with American ingredients like broccoli, tomatoes, carrots, and yellow onions, and fusing them with traditional Chinese cooking techniques like steaming, deep-frying, and stir-frying. As a result, foods like Sweet and Sour Chicken (page 102), Beef and Broccoli (page 118), and chop suey were invented here in America. Though they were not traditionally Chinese, they became staples in America, and a new type of cuisine was born.

Other Asian foods like Japanese, Korean, and Vietnamese, among others, followed a similar path. These immigrants brought their traditional cooking techniques and flavors, often out of necessity, and then fused them with American ingredients that were both popular and affordable. And as a result, many Asian American restaurants integrated their immigrant foods into popular mainstream America.

This book honors and celebrates many signature Asian dishes that we have all grown to enjoy. You'll discover fun food facts and new cooking techniques and learn how to use authentic seasonings, herbs, and sauces while fusing them with popular ingredients you can find in your local supermarket. Our *Easy Asian Cookbook* will help you master 100+ restaurant recipes in the comfort of your kitchen.

ONE
America Is a Crossroads for All Asian Foods

❀

America is a multicultural and multiracial country, with more than 45 million immigrants living in the United States today. We have more immigrants in America than any country in the world. And Asian Americans are the fastest growing group, making up 30 percent of the country's total immigrants.

Of course, Asia is a huge place with many histories, cultures, and foods. And thanks to that diversity, we enjoy a smorgasbord of Asian American dining that fuses many different traditional cooking techniques and flavors with American ingredients. This cookbook focuses on popular restaurant recipes that originated in Asia but were made in America. And in this sense, Asian restaurants are both great ambassadors and innovators of Asian food in the United States. They combine flavors and techniques from their origin with ingredients that can be found in supermarkets everywhere. And each immigrant community has enriched America with its food. Let's meet these Asian ambassadors!

Meet the Ambassadors of Asian Food in the United States

During the mid 19th and early 20th centuries, a great number of Asian immigrants moved to the United States in search of new opportunities. Today, a diverse mix of Asian people including, but certainly not limited to, the Chinese, Filipino, Japanese, Vietnamese, Korean, and Thai, among other communities, make up a large portion of immigrants who live in the United States.

For many immigrants, food is more than just a way to celebrate their heritage. Those who knew how to cook and prepare these dishes used it as a way to survive financially. In many cases, they opened restaurants and found ways to introduce their native foods to the American public, using American ingredients and making dishes more suitable to their palate. In other cases, immigrants opened up restaurants to cater more to their specific community, which introduced Americans to more authentic flavors of diverse cuisines. But as time went on, new generations of chefs started mixing together Western and Eastern influences. In the process, Asian American restaurateurs have created a variety of beloved fusion cuisines.

One popular example can be seen in the way Chinese restaurant owners took America's love of creamed corn and fused it with a traditional style of egg flower soup using cornstarch as a thickener. Restaurant patrons know this recipe today as Chicken Corn Soup (page 60). By comparison, Japanese restaurant owners took their style of teppanyaki cooking and added a beloved American ingredient—butter—to all their griddled dishes. This created the signature dish Hibachi Garlic Prawns (page 133), which tastes both new and familiar at the same time.

These days, it's fairly easy for us to order takeout and sample tasty signature dishes from faraway Asian countries that we may never get to travel to. But thanks to old and new Asian restaurants that pioneered and innovated their cuisines in America, we can now savor their most popular takeout dishes in the comfort of our homes.

CHINESE

Of all the Asian food ambassadors, the Chinese community—the largest Asian American community in the United States—led the way as the most popular type of Asian cooking. Chinese cuisine brought wok cooking and stir-fries to America and made them mainstream kitchen staples in kitchens everywhere. Dishes like Beef and Broccoli (page 118), Chicken Chow Mein (page 39), and Chicken Pot Stickers (page 26) introduced us to many signature flavors, cooking styles, and ingredients that were sometimes overlooked. Rice, soy sauce, ginger, scallions, chile paste, hoisin sauce, and oyster sauce are just a few of the many ingredients that Americans have grown to love.

FILIPINO

Although Filipino Americans make up the second largest Asian demographic in the United States, Filipino restaurants proliferated more slowly than some of their Asian counterparts. Of course, Filipino American food has existed as long as Filipino Americans have lived here, but it's only been in the last few years that the cuisine has started getting some of the recognition it deserves. The cuisine of the Philippines, a country of more than 7,000 islands, is already a fusion in and of itself. It has been occupied throughout history by many different countries, including China, Spain, and the United States. As a result, its cuisine is multifaceted, with influences from these countries as well as indigenous communities.

Filipino American chefs in Los Angeles, where there are more Filipinos than anywhere else outside of Manila, are often credited with accelerating the Filipino food movement. Young American-born chefs have been introducing fusion dishes to make their local food approachable. With hip décor and fancy plating, dishes like Chicken Adobo (page 108) and Sinigang (page 64) are on their way to becoming household names just like the many other dishes we are all familiar with now.

VIETNAMESE

Vietnamese migrants brought us pho, a noodle soup prepared with either beef, chicken, or seafood, that has become incredibly popular in recent years. These flavorful bone-broth soups have gained a cult-like following, but they aren't the only Vietnamese dishes to gain traction in the United States. Rice Noodles with Shrimp (page 44), Saigon Shrimp Spring Rolls (page 31), and Vietnamese Beef Stew (page 72), to name a few, are also widely available. The lightest cuisine of this bunch, Vietnamese food is a nice reprieve from the heavier cuisines that dominate the American diet. The hot climate of Vietnam molded its cuisine to be rice-based, and rice noodles often appear either in soup or tossed cold with grilled meats and tons of fresh herbs. The liberal use of fresh herbs and lime make this cuisine a healthier and lighter alternative to other Asian cuisines.

KOREAN

The sweet and spicy flavors of Korean food have made their mark in the United States in many different ways. Most prominently, Korean Americans introduced the country to their take on barbecue, where meats are marinated heavily in soy, sugar, garlic, and chiles, then grilled tableside and served with an array of small cold dishes called banchan. You can find Korean barbecue joints in most major cities, but that's not the only type of Korean food to go mainstream. Now, dishes like bulgogi (grilled slices of marinated beef or pork) and bibimbap (a rice bowl with lots of mix-ins) are regular items that you can find in food courts, restaurants, and food trucks from coast to coast. This book includes recipes for Pork Bulgogi (page 124) and Street Dog Bibimbap (page 52), among other favorites.

Unlike some other Asian restaurants, the first Korean restaurants in the United States catered primarily to Korean Americans and didn't try to attract others by changing flavors or ingredients. As a result, there aren't really Korean equivalents to pad Thai or orange chicken, dishes that were specifically created to appeal to Western palates. But that doesn't mean the chefs at some restaurants aren't making their own fusion dishes. These days, you can find traditional Korean ingredients, such as kimchi, in everything from burritos to tacos to hot dogs, and American diners are eating them up. All this attention has elevated the prominence of gochujang—a savory, sweet, spicy fermented Korean red chile paste—to the point where it is readily available in most ordinary supermarkets.

JAPANESE

Japanese cuisine has gained great popularity and has also earned a highly esteemed reputation for attention to detail, fine craftsmanship, and use of high-quality ingredients. It's not uncommon to fork over $150 or more for an omakase (chef's choice) meal at a high-end sushi spot in the United States. Japanese cuisine introduced a palatable way to eat raw fish through Americanized preparations. Creative rolls like Philly rolls, where cream cheese and raw salmon make a delightful combo, are common ways to get a new diner to try something different. And as our doors to new cuisines open wider, we become more adventurous, leading to more authentic ingredients and preparations of sashimi and sushi. Americans chowing down on toro (a high-grade cut of tuna), amaebi (sweet shrimp), and uni (sea urchin) with complete joy is now a common sight at sushi bars.

Sushi and sashimi tend to be most abundant and of the highest caliber in major cities, but small towns have their share of restaurants serving simpler Japanese American fare such as Teriyaki Chicken (page 105) and Miso Soup (page 69). Also popular are restaurants specializing in teppanyaki cooking (also called "hibachi-style" in the United States), in which food is cooked on an iron griddle, often in front of customers. Ramen joints, which serve a variety of noodle soups, have also proliferated in recent years. This book includes recipes for Hibachi Garlic Prawns (page 133) and Shoyu Pork Corn Ramen (page 49) to satiate your appetite for these favorites.

The variety of Japanese food is vast, but one thing is consistent among its dishes: The food isn't particularly spicy, sour, or sweet. The flavors are simple and pure, which may be one reason why it translated so well to the American palate.

THAI AND OTHER GROUPS

Despite the relatively small population of Thai Americans living in the United States compared to other Asian groups, Thai restaurants have a big presence across the United States. During its first introduction to the country, Thai restaurant food often catered to the Western palate with menus composed of noodle or rice dishes that used sugar with a heavy hand. Dishes such as Pad Thai with Tofu (page 54), Drunken Noodles with Chicken (page 46), and Street-Style Chicken Satay (page 29) became stalwarts of Thai cuisine, though they were not necessarily authentic.

Now you can venture into Thai Town in Los Angeles or head to Portland's famous Thai spot Pok Pok to get more authentic flavors that combine spicy, sweet, salty, sour, and bitter all in the same dish, using ingredients such as spice, lime, rice powder, and fish sauce.

As Americans welcome different flavor profiles, other Asian cuisines—Malaysian, Indonesian, Cambodian, Myanmarese, and Sri Lankan, to name a few—are making their way into the American restaurant scene. This book provides a taste of those cuisines as well, with dishes such as Curry Potato Samosas (page 33), from Myanmar, and Parippu (page 96), a red lentil curry from Sri Lanka.

Largest Asian Populations by US City

1 NEW YORK: CHINESE. The cuisine is heavily based on stir-fries seasoned with soy sauce, ginger, garlic, and scallions. Mongolian Beef (page 117) and Kung Pao Chicken (page 103) are two wok dishes representative of this group.

2 DALY CITY, CA: FILIPINO. The cuisine has a mix of influences from other cultures, ranging from Spanish, Portuguese, and Chinese to American. It's heavily based in pork, chicken, and seafood dishes, many of which are cooked with garlic, onions, tomatoes, carrots, and potatoes in a stew-like fashion. Chicken Adobo (page 108) and Lumpia (page 30) are favorites in the United States.

3 ORANGE COUNTY, CA: VIETNAMESE. Known to be much lighter than other Asian cuisines, Vietnamese food is largely focused on rice-based noodles served in soups or tossed cold as a salad, as well as grilled dishes wrapped in lettuce, aromatics, and fresh herbs. Many Vietnamese dishes use light dressings made from fish sauce, lime juice, and chile. Pho Ga (Hanoi Chicken Pho, page 43), Shaking Beef (page 122), and Saigon Shrimp Spring Rolls (page 31) are great examples of popular Vietnamese dishes.

4 LOS ANGELES: KOREAN. Korean cuisine is meat-based with many dishes marinated in chiles, soy, fermented chile paste, and pulsed fruit. In addition to barbecue meats and stews, Korean food is also known for its many pickled and fermented vegetable side dishes called banchan. Kimchi Army Stew (page 63) highlights kimchi, which is made with cabbage and is perhaps the most popular of the Korean fermented delights.

5 HONOLULU: **JAPANESE.** Japanese cuisine comes in many different forms including sushi, ramen, tempura, and curry. Hawaii has a long history with Japanese immigrants, and their influence can be seen in the cuisine. Recently, a version of poke has exploded onto the restaurant scene on the mainland. In Hawaii, poke is typically a marinated raw fish dish served with various condiments of Japanese influence. In the United States, poke is often made with tuna and served in a bowl with nontraditional ingredients. This book includes a recipe for Tuna Poke Bowl (page 134).

6 LOS ANGELES: **THAI.** Thai food has a huge Chinese influence, as it has many similar stir-fried dishes. However, the flavor profiles differ. Rather than a focus on soy sauce, garlic, and ginger, Thai stir-fries make use of fish sauce, shrimp paste, chile, lemongrass, and tamarind. Salads and curries are also distinctive in Thai cuisine and are heavily coconut-based, unlike many other Asian cuisines. Check out Green Papaya Salad (page 93) and Thai Basil Chicken (page 109), to try some favorites.

Build Your Asian Food Pantry

If you're going to start cooking Asian takeout at home, you'll need to stock a pantry. Here's a list to get you started.

BASIC INGREDIENTS

Chile oil: This is oil that has been simmered with dried chile flakes. It's used to cook with and added to dishes for a kick of spice. Make your own or find it at Asian markets or in the Asian section of most supermarkets.

Chile powder: This spice is made from a single type of ground dried chile. They all have slightly different tastes and heat levels. Don't confuse this with "Chili powder seasoning," which is a spice blend (usually with dried chiles, garlic, oregano, and cumin) primarily used to season chili, the bean-and-meat stew. Find common chile powders at any supermarket or look online for less common ones, such as gochugaru, Korean chile powder; and shichi-mi togarashi, Japanese seven-flavor chile powder.

Coconut milk: Widely used in soups and curries to create a creamy texture. It typically comes in cans or cartons. Always use full-fat coconut milk for a richer flavor. Find it in the Asian section of most supermarkets.

Cornstarch: A flavorless and opaque powder. It's often used as a thickening agent in Asian sauces, soups, stews, curries, and stir-fries by making a whisked "slurry" of equal parts water and cornstarch. Also used for marinating proteins before stir-frying. Find it in the baking section of any supermarket.

Dried chile flakes: Adds mild heat to sauces, marinades, curries, and soups. Not to be confused with chile powder (ground dried chiles) which is spicier. Often labeled "red pepper flakes." Find it in the spice section of any supermarket.

Fish sauce: A pungent seasoning made from anchovy and salt. It adds depth to a dish by bringing in a balance of salt and umami. Find it in the Asian section of any supermarket.

Hoisin sauce: A rich, thick sauce that's salty and sweet. Can be seen as the "Asian barbecue sauce," but less sweet and minus the smokiness. Find it in the Asian section of any supermarket and get the Lee Kum Kee brand.

Rice (long-grain or short-grain): Rice is the staple food of Asia. Southeast Asian and Chinese cuisines usually call for long-grain rice, which is aromatic, firm, light, and fluffy, while Japanese cuisine often calls for short-grain rice, which is slightly sticky, firmer, and chewy. You can use either type when recipes call for white rice. Some recipes call for jasmine rice, which is a fragrant type of long-grain rice, or sweet rice, a type of short-grain rice also called "glutinous rice." Find them in the Asian section of any supermarket (and see my Steamed Rice recipe, page 19).

Rice noodles (thin or wide): Noodles made from rice flour and water. They have a slippery, smooth, and sometimes springy feel and are widely used in Southeast Asia and Southern China. Can be eaten in soup or tossed with sauces as a salad. Find them in the Asian section of any supermarket.

Soy sauce: Originated in China and is now used in most Asian cuisines. It is made from fermented soybeans and tastes salty and slightly sweet, with an umami flavor. Soy sauce has become mainstream and is readily available in any supermarket.

Sriracha: A thick, salty, garlicky, slightly acidic, and slightly sweet chile sauce that originated in Thailand. This globally popular hot sauce can be found at any supermarket.

Toasted sesame oil: Rich and nutty in flavor with a strong fragrant aroma. It is used in dressings, sauces, marinades, or as a seasoning. Find it in Asian markets, high-end grocery stores, and online.

Turmeric powder: This bright orange-yellow powder used in curries, marinades, soups, and sauces adds hints of ginger, orange, and musk to dishes. Find it in the spice section of any supermarket.

OPTIONAL INGREDIENTS

Black vinegar (chinkiang): Similar to balsamic vinegar, except less sweet and with a bit of savory umami. Used as a dipping sauce for dumplings and to make sauces for noodles, stir-fries, and stews. Find it at Asian markets or online. *Substitute with a dry balsamic that hasn't been aged for long.*

Curry paste: Made from ground curry powder, ginger, garlic, salt, and herbs. It's used as a marinade and a base for curry recipes and soups. This book calls for different types, such as red or yellow. Find them all in the Asian section of any supermarket or an Asian market. *Substitute with a mixture of turmeric powder, dried chile flakes, coriander seeds, and cumin that has been toasted in oil over medium heat for 1 minute.*

Dark soy sauce: Used mostly in Chinese dishes, it's an aged soy that contains caramel and molasses, which make it thicker, darker, and more robust in flavor than regular soy. Find it in Asian markets or online. *Substitute with regular soy sauce.*

Gochujang: A slightly sweet Korean chile sauce made from fermented soybeans, glutinous rice, and chiles. Used as a seasoning, a marinade, or a component of sauces. Find it at high-end groceries or an Asian market. *Substitute with a mix of sriracha and honey.*

Kimchi: Vegetables fermented with salt, chiles, seafood, and various aromatics. The most common kimchi is made from Napa cabbage. Find at high-end groceries and Asian markets. *Substitute by marinating shredded cabbage with salt, sugar, fish sauce, dried chile flakes, sriracha, garlic, and onions.*

Lemongrass paste: Used when fresh lemongrass is not available. Adds a fresh lemon-lime-ginger aroma and taste to dishes. Widely used in Southeast Asia and Sri Lanka. Can be found at Asian markets or online. *Substitute with lime juice and zest.*

Mirin: Mirin is a subtly sweet, low-alcohol wine made from glutinous rice that is a staple in Japanese cooking. Similar to sake, though higher in sugar, it's used to add sweetness and flavors to a variety of dishes, sauces, and glazes. Sometimes, it's simply called "rice wine." Find it in the Asian section of most supermarkets, in Asian markets, and online. *Substitute with dry white wine.*

Miso: A Japanese seasoning made from fermented soybeans, salt, grains, and other ingredients. There are various types of miso pastes, such as red, white, and brown. Used as a base for soups, marinades, and sauces. Find it at Asian markets or online. *Substitute with soy sauce and tahini.*

Oyster sauce: A sweet, salty, and rich sauce made from oysters, sugar, and salt. This thick, savory, caramel-like seasoning is used in Chinese, Thai, Vietnamese, and Malay cuisines. Find it at Asian markets or online. *Substitute with a mix of soy sauce and hoisin sauce.*

Sake: Japanese rice wine that comes in dry and sweet versions. Find it at high-end groceries and Asian markets. *Substitute with dry white wine.*

Shrimp paste: Made from fermented crushed shrimp with salt and used in soups, curries, and sauces. Find it at Asian markets and online. *Substitute with small amounts of anchovy paste.*

Tamarind paste: Made from tamarind pods to add a sour flavor to dishes. Used in Filipino, Thai, and other Southeast Asian cuisines. Find it at Asian markets or online. *Substitute with equal parts lime juice and brown sugar.*

FUN ASIAN FOOD FACT

Gourmands and historians will tell you that food not only shapes your present and future, but it also molded your past. And when it comes to Asian cuisine, these three foods played an important part in the region and determined the fate of many people all over the world.

Rice is one of the oldest foods, a pillar of nutrition that helped humanity evolve from a hunting and gathering society to a farming one. Asia alone grows and eats 90 percent of the world's rice. And the Chinese even used rice to build some of their most famous monuments—The Great Wall of China is partially held together with sticky rice! This cookbook features 8 rice dishes, and 33 main dishes are served with rice.

Sesame oil is an excellent source of nutrition. Many consider sesame seeds a superfood that is good for hair and skin, and they help reduce stress and anxiety. This cookbook features 28 sesame oil recipes, ranging from comfort foods like Wonton Soup (page 61) to healthy vegetable dishes like Sesame Bean Sprouts (page 88) and Cold Tofu with Scallions (page 79).

Pork is a signature ingredient in Asia, highly esteemed for taste, texture, and color. And for many Chinese, this food is also part of their philosophy. Confucius is credited with saying that the way you cut your meat reflects the way you live. And from pork loin to pork belly and pork shoulder, these cuts have shaped Asian cuisine since antiquity. This cookbook features 13 pork recipes and 23 dishes that can be made with pork.

Know Your Kitchen Tools

These are the common kitchen tools you'll use often when making recipes in this cookbook. While they are highly recommended and used in the recipes here, you can sometimes substitute them with a more common piece of kitchen equipment.

Cast-iron skillet: The ability to retain high, consistent heat makes a skillet desirable for all your frying needs.

Chopsticks: Use chopsticks to mix, whisk, stir-fry, and pick up food. They're a versatile tool that can be used for everything. *Substitute with a standard fork for mixing and whisking, a flat wooden spatula for stir-frying, and tongs to pick up food.*

Clay pot: Many braises, stews, and curries are made in a clay pot. It retains greater heat for longer periods of time and is often served directly on the table once the dish is done cooking. *Substitute with a Dutch oven or enameled cast-iron pot.*

Food processor: This everyday kitchen gadget is extremely useful for mixing, blending, and pulsing ingredients into pastes or sauces.

Large stockpot: Every kitchen should be equipped with a large, heavy-bottomed stockpot for boiling and for making soups and broths.

Mandoline: This handy tool helps you slice vegetables thinly and quickly. *Substitute with a chef's knife (and practice with patience!) or purchase shredded or precut vegetables.*

Nonstick wok: A workhorse in the Asian kitchen, the wok is used for stir-frying, shallow-frying, steaming, and sautéing. A 14-inch wok is a great size to start with. Almost every dish (except soups, stews, and braises) can be prepared in a wok. *Substitute with a cast-iron skillet or nonstick sauté pan.*

Rice cooker: Most households that eat rice on a daily basis have a rice cooker. It prepares rice perfectly, can be left alone to cook without monitoring, and can keep rice warm for later use. *Substitute with a saucepot on the stovetop. See page 19 for my stovetop method.*

Saucepot: Smaller than a stockpot, this pot can handle recipes for soups, curries, and boiling.

Stainless steel steamer stack and pot set: Steamer stacks are commonly used in Chinese cuisine for steaming seafood, dumplings, dim sum, proteins, and vegetables. A full steamer stack and pot set can take up cupboard space and be costly, especially if you only use it for steaming. *Substitute with a simple steam rack placed in a large stockpot with water filled halfway to the rack. Place a flat plate or shallow bowl on the rack, and you are ready to steam.*

Polish Your Cooking Techniques

This book uses a few common cooking techniques again and again. Here's what you need to know to successfully complete each.

Boiling: Bring a large pot of water to a boil over high heat, then add the ingredients and cook until tender.

Braising: First sauté or sear the ingredients with oil in a clay pot or Dutch oven over high heat. Then add the liquid, such as stock, to the pot. Reduce the heat to low, cover the pot, and simmer the ingredients for the time specified to allow the flavors to build, ingredients to tenderize, and liquid to be reduced.

Deep-frying: Place 3 to 4 inches of oil in a wok or cast-iron skillet and heat it over high heat to 375°F. Once the oil is hot, add the ingredients and cook until golden brown. Sometimes, you must work in batches because crowding the wok can cool the oil too much and affect cooking.

Pan-frying: Heat a sauté pan or skillet over high heat, then add a small amount of oil. Add the ingredients and cook on each side until golden brown or fully cooked. When pan-frying dumplings, water and oil are added to the skillet with a lid on. Once the water evaporates, oil sears the bottom of the dumplings to a golden crisp.

Shallow-frying: Place 1 inch of oil in a wok or cast-iron skillet and heat over medium heat. Add the ingredients and cook until golden brown on both sides. This technique lets you control doneness more than deep-frying, as it uses a lower heat level.

Steaming: This is the healthiest method of cooking. Add water to a steamer pot or pan so that it only comes halfway up to the steam rack. Add the rack and set the pot over high heat. When the water boils, place ingredients in the steamer or on a plate on the steam rack (see page 15). Reduce the heat to medium, cover the pot, and cook until tender. Remember, the ingredient itself does not touch water. The boiling water vaporizes into a hot steam that cooks the food.

Stir-frying: Heat a wok or cast-iron skillet over high heat. Add a small amount of oil and move the wok in a circular motion to coat its surface with oil. Once the oil is hot, add the ingredients and cook, still over high heat and stirring constantly. It's a quick process, and the order in which you work is important. Aromatics such as ginger, garlic, scallions, spices are always added first, then proteins, then vegetables last. Typically, a stir-fry is finished with a slurry of cornstarch and water, which thickens the sauce created in the wok.

About the Recipes

This book was written to be an easy cookbook that introduces you to common Asian ingredients and techniques. However, it's not meant to be an authentic or comprehensive resource to all Asian cuisine—one book could surely never do justice to such a multifaceted subject. That's why these recipes focus on new and old restaurant favorites that originated in Asia or were inspired by Asian cooking, but which were reinvented or created in the United States.

While the recipes highlight Asian ingredients and kitchen equipment, remember that you can always refer to the ingredient list (page 9) and kitchen tools list (page 14) in this chapter to find substitutes and alternatives.

Each recipe includes labels to help you find the dishes you'd like to make. These include:

- ✿ Country of origin or inspiration

- ✿ Dietary options (Gluten-free, Nut-free, Soy-free, Vegetarian)

- ✿ Indicators of ease and time

  - **5 INGREDIENTS** (uses five ingredients or less, excluding salt, pepper, water, and oil)

  - **FASTER THAN DELIVERY** (can be made in 45 minutes or less)

  - **ONE POT** (the entire recipe can be made in one pot or pan)

  - **TAKEOUT FAVORITE** (the most popular dishes at Asian restaurants)

Many recipes also include cooking, ingredient, and substitution tips to make your time in the kitchen as easy as possible. Let's get cooking!

Steamed Rice

GLUTEN-FREE ❀ NUT-FREE ❀ SOY-FREE ❀ VEGETARIAN
5 INGREDIENTS ❀ FASTER THAN DELIVERY ❀ TAKEOUT FAVORITE

If you don't have a rice cooker, you can make rice on the stovetop. This is a basic recipe for medium-grain rice. Cooking time and rice-to-water ratio can sometimes vary depending on your stove's heat level and the brand of rice. It may take a couple tries to get your rice perfect, but this is a good place to start.

SERVES 4
PREP TIME: 5 minutes
COOK TIME: 20 minutes

2 cups medium-grain
white rice
2¾ cups water

1. Rinse the rice under cold water and drain. Repeat this process until the water runs clear; usually 2 to 3 times is enough.

2. Combine the rice and the water in a saucepan that has a tight-fitting lid. Turn the heat to high, cover the pan, and bring to a boil.

3. Immediately reduce the heat to low and simmer for 10 minutes, or until the water has been absorbed. Don't lift the lid while it cooks. Remove from the heat and set aside to rest for 10 minutes with the lid still on.

4. Remove the lid and fluff the rice with a fork or chopsticks. Serve.

Largest Asian Food Communities in the U.S.

This map includes some of the
cities with the largest Asian
communities and some dishes
from those communities
featured in the book.

SEATTLE
JAPANESE: Shoyu Pork
Corn Ramen (page 49)

SACRAMENTO
JAPANESE: Hibachi
Garlic Prawns
(page 133)

DALY CITY
FILIPINO:
Chicken Adobo
(page 108)

SAN FRANCISCO
CHINESE: Red Oil
Tossed Pork Wontons
(page 25)
FILIPINO: Fried
Tilapia with Salsa
(page 138)
JAPANESE: Chicken
Katsu Curry (page 70)

SAN JOSE
CHINESE: Pumpkin Rice Cake
(page 148)
JAPANESE: Miso Soup (page 69)
VIETNAMESE: Saigon Shrimp
Spring Rolls (page 31)

FREMONT
CHINESE: Kung Pao
Chicken (page 103)
FILIPINO: Sinigang
(page 64)
KOREAN: Pork
Bulgogi (page 124)

LOS ANGELES
CAMBODIAN: Pork
Curry (page 71)
FILIPINO: Lumpia
(page 30)
INDONESIAN: Mie
Goreng (page 53)
JAPANESE: Pineapple
Yakult Ice Pops (page 146)
KOREAN: Korean Short
Rib Soup (Galbitang)
(page 62)
THAI: Drunken
Noodles (page 46)

SAN DIEGO
FILIPINO: Filipino
Chocolate Rice Pudding
(Champorado) (page 150)
KOREAN: Street Dog
Bibimbap (page 52)
THAI: Street-Style
Chicken Satay (page 29)
VIETNAMESE:
Vietnamese Beef Stew
(Bò Kho) (page 72)

HONOLULU
CHINESE: Beef
and Broccoli
(page 118)
FILIPINO: Chicken
Kare Kare (page 65)
JAPANESE: Teriyaki
Chicken (page 105)

MINNEAPOLIS-ST. PAUL

MYANMARESE: Curry Potato Samosas (page 33)

CHICAGO

CHINESE: Chicken Chow Mein (page 39)
JAPANESE: Shoyu Pork Corn Ramen (page 49)
KOREAN: Japchae (page 51)

INDIANAPOLIS

MYANMARESE: Mint Chicken (page 110)

NEW YORK

CHINESE: Mapo Tofu with Pork (page 120)
INDONESIAN: Crispy Tofu with Peanut Sauce (page 95)
KOREAN: Sesame Bean Sprouts (page 88)
MALAYSIAN: Lamb Rendang (page 73)
SRI LANKAN: Red Lentil Curry (Parippu) (page 96)
THAI: Pad Thai with Tofu (page 54)

HOUSTON

CHINESE: Chicken Pot Stickers (page 26)
KOREAN: Kimchi Army Stew (Budae Jijigae) (page 63)

PHILADELPHIA

CHINESE: Honey Walnut Shrimp (page 131)
KOREAN: Sweet and Spicy Korean Short Ribs (Galbi) (page 125)
VIETNAMESE: Rice Noodles with Shrimp (Bún Chả) (page 44)

STREET-STYLE CHICKEN SATAY, PAGE 29

TWO
Appetizers

❀

Red Oil Tossed Pork Wontons 25

Chicken Pot Stickers (Guōtiē) 26

Minced Chicken Lettuce Wraps 27

Shrimp Toast 28

Street-Style Chicken Satay 29

Lumpia 30

Saigon Shrimp Spring Rolls 31

Kimchi Scallion Pancakes 32

Curry Potato Samosas 33

Crab Rangoon 34

Appetizers are often the most exciting part of the meal.
They entice diners and give them a preview of what's to come. Appetizers are meant to be shared in Asian culture, which means that you can enjoy a wide variety of textures and flavors in the appetizer courses alone. There are steamed, boiled, deep-fried, and pan-fried appetizers, and then there are sweet, spicy, tangy, and savory flavors. In this chapter, you will learn to make some of the most popular Asian appetizers we've all come to love. Many of these recipes not only are easy to make but can be made faster than you can get them ordered and delivered from a restaurant.

FUN ASIAN FOOD FACT

The word *wonton* has several literal meanings, depending on which region of China you are referring to. "Cloud swallow," "crossed hands," and "chaos" are a few of the word's literal meanings. Each region in China has its own version of wontons, which are wrapped in various shapes and prepared with different fillings. They can also be eaten in different ways—steamed, boiled, in soup, tossed, or pan-fried. Red Oil Tossed Pork Wontons (page 25) hail from the Sichuan region of China and are served tossed in a spicy chile oil sauce. In Shanghai, wontons are larger than in Sichuan and are served in a rich chicken broth or pan-fried. In Cantonese cuisine, wontons are much more delicate. Shrimp or pork filling is wrapped in thin wrappers and served floating in a light broth made from dried shrimp and pork bone.

Red Oil Tossed Pork Wontons

NUT-FREE

These wontons hail from the Sichuan Province, where wontons are usually filled with pork and tossed in sauce, not served in soup as is common in other areas. To speed things up, flavorful Italian sausage is used in this recipe instead of ground pork.

MAKES 20 wontons
PREP TIME: 15 minutes
COOK TIME: 8 minutes

¾ pound Italian sausage

1 teaspoon minced ginger

2 tablespoons toasted sesame oil

20 square wonton wrappers

½ cup chile oil

1 tablespoon dried chile flakes

3 tablespoons soy sauce

1 tablespoon black vinegar

1. To make the filling, mix together the sausage, ginger, and sesame oil in a bowl.

2. Place one wrapper on the palm of your hand. Add 1 teaspoon of filling to the center. Dip your finger in water and wet two edges of the wrapper. Fold the wrapper over to form a triangle. Press out the air, then press the edges to seal. Dab water on the left corner, place the right corner over the left corner, and press down.

3. Repeat this process with the remaining filling and wrappers.

4. Bring a large pot of water to a boil over high heat. Add the wontons and cook until they float, then cook for 30 more seconds. Transfer the wontons to a bowl with a slotted spoon.

5. Whisk together the chile oil, chile flakes, soy sauce, and vinegar, then pour the sauce over the wontons and serve.

SWAP IT: Substitute the black vinegar with balsamic vinegar.

Chicken Pot Stickers (Guōtiē)

NUT-FREE ❀ FASTER THAN DELIVERY ❀ TAKEOUT FAVORITE

The phrase *guō tiē* literally means "wok stick" in Mandarin. Many believe pot stickers were an accidental creation. It's said that the Imperial chef of the Song Dynasty boiled the water dry in his wok, causing his dumplings to stick to it. After peeling them off and discovering a delightful crisp texture, he served the dish, and it became a hit.

MAKES 20 pot stickers
PREP TIME: 15 minutes
COOK TIME: 10 minutes

½ pound ground chicken

¼ cup finely chopped celery

¼ cup finely chopped
    scallions

3 tablespoons soy sauce

1 teaspoon sugar

1 teaspoon cornstarch

1 tablespoon toasted
    sesame oil

20 round
    dumpling wrappers

⅓ cup water

1 tablespoon canola oil

1. To make the filling, mix together the chicken, celery, scallions, soy sauce, sugar, cornstarch, and sesame oil in a bowl.

2. Place one wrapper on the palm of your hand. Add 1 teaspoon of filling to the center. Dip your finger in water and wet the bottom-half edge of the wrapper. Fold the wrapper over to form a half-circle. Press out the air, then press the edges to seal.

3. Repeat this process with the remaining filling and wrappers.

4. In a nonstick pan over high heat, pour in the water and dumplings. Cover the pan and cook until the water is absorbed, 6 to 8 minutes. Work in batches if needed; do not overcrowd the pan.

5. Add the canola oil to the pan and fry the dumplings until golden brown, about 2 minutes.

6. If working in batches, remove the dumplings and cook the next batch in a clean pan.

SERVING TIP: Buy gyoza sauce for pot stickers or make your own by mixing soy sauce with vinegar, sriracha, and sesame oil.

Minced Chicken Lettuce Wraps

NUT-FREE ❁ FASTER THAN DELIVERY ❁ TAKEOUT FAVORITE

Lettuce wraps have become popular in the last decade due to low-carb diets, but they were a favorite dish on Chinese American restaurant menus long before that. In Cantonese, lettuce wraps are called *sang choy bao*.

SERVES 4
PREP TIME: 10 minutes
COOK TIME: 8 minutes

¾ pound ground chicken

2 tablespoons soy
    sauce, divided

2 teaspoons cornstarch,
    divided

1 teaspoon sugar

1 tablespoon toasted
    sesame oil

1 teaspoon salt, divided

1 head romaine lettuce

1 tablespoon canola oil

1 large zucchini,
    finely chopped

1 red bell pepper,
    finely chopped

2 tablespoons hoisin sauce

1 teaspoon water

1. In a bowl, combine the chicken with 1 tablespoon of soy sauce, 1 teaspoon of cornstarch, the sugar, sesame oil, and ½ teaspoon of salt and marinate for 5 minutes.

2. Peel the romaine leaves off the core, rinse them, and let them air dry.

3. In a wok over high heat, pour in the canola oil. Add the marinated chicken, zucchini, and bell pepper and stir-fry for 5 minutes.

4. Add the remaining ½ teaspoon of salt, the remaining 1 tablespoon of soy sauce, and the hoisin sauce and stir-fry for 2 minutes.

5. Mix the water with the remaining 1 teaspoon of cornstarch to make a slurry. Add it to the wok and stir-fry for 1 minute.

6. Place the filling in the romaine leaves and serve.

SERVING TIP: For added crunch, sprinkle sliced almonds or candied peanuts on top.

Shrimp Toast

NUT-FREE ✿ FASTER THAN DELIVERY ✿ TAKEOUT FAVORITE

Shrimp toast originated from the Guangdong Province more than 100 years ago. It's commonly served at dim sum restaurants. Shrimp toast is called "hai tosi" in Cantonese, with *hai* meaning "shrimp" and *tosi* meaning "toast."

MAKES 12 pieces
PREP TIME: 10 minutes
COOK TIME: 8 minutes

10 medium shrimp, peeled and deveined

½ teaspoon garlic salt

½ teaspoon sugar

½ cup finely chopped scallions

1 teaspoon toasted sesame oil

1 egg white

¼ cup black sesame seeds

3 white bread slices, toasted, crusts removed, and quartered

3 tablespoons canola oil

1. In a food processor or blender, combine the shrimp, garlic salt, sugar, scallions, sesame oil, and egg white and pulse until a smooth paste forms.

2. Pour the sesame seeds onto a plate.

3. Spread 1 tablespoon of shrimp paste on each triangle of toast.

4. Roll each triangle, paste-side down, into sesame seeds to coat.

5. Heat the canola oil in a nonstick sauté pan or skillet over medium heat. Add the toast, sesame-side down, and cook on each side for 2 minutes, or until golden brown.

SWAP IT: Substitute black sesame seeds with white sesame seeds or poppy seeds.

Street-Style Chicken Satay

GLUTEN-FREE ❀ SOY-FREE ❀ ONE POT ❀ TAKEOUT FAVORITE

Although satay can be found on Asian menus of all stripes, the Thai version is likely the most popular, given the number of Thai restaurants in the United States. But the Javanese from Indonesia are the ones who first created satay, thanks to the influence of the Arabs who immigrated to Java and brought their kebabs along with them.

SERVES 4
PREP TIME: 10 minutes, plus 1 hour to marinate
COOK TIME: 8 minutes

2 tablespoons chopped lemongrass or lime juice

1 tablespoon minced ginger

1 teaspoon cumin

1 teaspoon turmeric

3 tablespoons fish sauce

2 tablespoons sugar

2 tablespoons chunky peanut butter

1 pound chicken tenders

2 tablespoons coconut oil, melted, or canola oil

1. In a blender, combine the lemongrass, ginger, cumin, turmeric, fish sauce, sugar, and peanut butter and pulse together. Transfer to a zip-top bag, then add the chicken. Close the bag and squeeze to coat the chicken evenly. Marinate for 1 hour or overnight.

2. Meanwhile, soak 10 to 12 skewers in water for 1 hour.

3. Thread the marinated chicken on the skewers, and brush the skewered chicken on both sides with the oil. Place the skewers on a hot grill, and cook for 4 minutes on each side, or until the chicken juices run clear. Alternatively, broil the chicken for about 10 minutes. Serve.

SERVING TIP: Make a peanut dipping sauce by mixing chunky peanut butter with coconut milk, fish sauce, honey, and sambal (an Indonesian chile paste) in a blender.

Lumpia

NUT-FREE ❁ SOY-FREE ❁ FASTER THAN DELIVERY ❁ TAKEOUT FAVORITE

Lumpia are the Filipino take on egg rolls. Their wrappers are lighter than spring roll or egg roll wrappers, and they are longer and slenderer in shape than either of those appetizers. This makes for a light and crispy snack.

MAKES 12 pieces
PREP TIME: 20 minutes
COOK TIME: 8 minutes

1 cup canola oil, divided

¾ pound ground pork

½ cup finely
    shredded carrots

½ teaspoon salt

½ teaspoon sugar

1 tablespoon toasted
    sesame oil

½ teaspoon freshly ground
    black pepper

12 lumpia or spring
    roll wrappers

2 eggs, whisked

1. In a wok over high heat, pour in 1 teaspoon of canola oil. Add the pork, carrots, salt, sugar, sesame oil, and pepper and stir-fry for 3 minutes. Remove from the heat and let the filling cool for 10 minutes.

2. Lay a wrapper on a work surface with a corner pointing toward you. Place 2 tablespoons of filling in the center. Fold the corner closest to you over the filling to cover. Fold the left and right corners over the filling, then roll up until the top corner is reached. Dab some of the egg on the top corner to seal.

3. Repeat this process with the remaining filling and wrappers.

4. Heat the remaining canola oil in a Dutch oven over high heat to 340°F. Use a deep-fry thermometer to check the temperature.

5. Add the lumpia to the canola oil and deep-fry until golden brown, about 8 minutes. Transfer the lumpia to paper towels to drain, then serve.

> **SWAP IT:** For a fun twist, swap the pork filling for cheese sticks. Roll the wrappers around cheese sticks, freeze, and then fry over low to medium heat. This is called "lumpiang keso."

Saigon Shrimp Spring Rolls

GLUTEN-FREE ✿ NUT-FREE ✿ FASTER THAN DELIVERY ✿ TAKEOUT FAVORITE

Spring rolls are called "gỏi cuốn" in Vietnamese. Stuffed with rice vermicelli, pork, beef, shrimp, or tofu, they provide a nice contrast to heavier appetizers, since they aren't fried. You may see these called "summer rolls" or "salad rolls" on menus. This version uses fresh vegetables and fruit for an even healthier take.

MAKES 12 pieces
PREP TIME: 20 minutes

3 cups water

3 cups coleslaw mix

1 cup diced pineapple

¼ cup apple cider vinegar

¼ cup maple syrup

½ teaspoon salt

1 tablespoon fish sauce

12 spring roll wrappers

12 medium prawns, shelled, boiled, and halved

1. In a saucepot over high heat, bring the water to a boil.

2. In a bowl, mix together the coleslaw mix, pineapple, vinegar, maple syrup, salt, and fish sauce.

3. Dip one wrapper in the hot water for 1 second to soften. Place it flat on a cutting board. Add 2 tablespoons of filling to the center, then top with two pieces of prawn. Fold the right side over the filling, then fold the left side over the filling. Fold the bottom over filling and continue to roll tightly until you reach the top of the wrapper to seal.

4. Repeat this process with the remaining filling and wrappers and serve.

SERVING TIP: Serve spring rolls with a side of hoisin sauce for dipping and add herbs for more color and freshness.

Kimchi Scallion Pancakes

NUT-FREE ❁ VEGETARIAN ❁ FASTER THAN DELIVERY

These savory pancakes can be whipped up in 20 minutes. Serve them for breakfast, lunch, or dinner as a side or snack. The addition of kimchi gives an extra kick of flavor to the traditional Korean scallion pancake, *pa jun*.

SERVES 4
PREP TIME: 10 minutes
COOK TIME: 10 minutes

1½ cups all-purpose flour

½ cup rice flour

2 eggs, beaten

1½ cups water

½ cup chopped
  store-bought kimchi

1 cup chopped scallions

1 teaspoon salt

4 teaspoons canola oil

1. In a large bowl, pour in the all-purpose flour, rice flour, eggs, water, kimchi, scallions, and salt and whisk together until a smooth batter forms. Let it sit for 5 minutes.

2. In a small nonstick sauté pan or skillet, pour in 1 teaspoon of oil and heat on high. Pour ⅓ cup of batter into the skillet, reduce the heat to medium, and cook on each side for 3 minutes, or until golden brown. Transfer to a plate.

3. Repeat this process with the remaining 3 teaspoons of oil and batter. Serve.

SWAP IT: If rice flour is unavailable, use all-purpose flour, 2 cups total.

SERVING TIP: Serve with a dipping sauce of soy sauce mixed with a few drops of sesame oil. Add chia seeds into the batter for a healthy, pretty twist.

Curry Potato Samosas

SOY-FREE ❁ VEGETARIAN

Samosas are called *samusas* in Myanmar. However, the true origins of samosas are traced to Central Asia and the Middle East. Many styles emerged: baked or fried, spiced, nutty, and fruity. This version hails from Myanmar and can be made in a flash thanks to Instant mashed potatoes.

MAKES 12 pieces
PREP TIME: 10 minutes
COOK TIME: 10 minutes

4 tablespoons butter

1 tablespoon turmeric

2 cups store-bought chicken broth

½ teaspoon salt

¼ teaspoon sugar

1 teaspoon garlic powder

1½ cups instant mashed potato flakes

2 sheets frozen puff pastry, thawed

2 egg yolks, beaten

1. Preheat the oven to 400°F.

2. In a saucepan over high heat, melt the butter. Add the turmeric and cook for 10 seconds.

3. Whisk in the broth, salt, sugar, and garlic powder and bring to a boil.

4. Slowly whisk in the potato flakes. Let the potato absorb the broth and hydrate into a mashed potato consistency.

5. Unroll the puff pastry and let it sit out for 2 minutes, then cut it into 2-inch squares.

6. Fill the center of each square with 1 tablespoon of potato filling. Dab egg yolk along 2 edges. Fold one corner to the opposite corner to form a triangle. Press out the air and seal.

7. Transfer the samosas to a baking sheet and bake for 10 minutes, or until golden brown.

SERVING TIP: For a crispier take on samosas, use egg roll wrappers and deep-fry them.

Crab Rangoon

**NUT-FREE ✿ 5 INGREDIENTS ✿ FASTER THAN DELIVERY
TAKEOUT FAVORITE**

Cream cheese became a staple between 1940 and 1950, which coincides with the growth of tiki culture. This dish may have been invented by Victor Bergeron, Jr., the founder of the famous Trader Vic's tiki bars during the early 1940s. Rangoon is actually a city in Myanmar (formerly known as Burma), now called Yangon. While the name is Myanmarese, the dish is Chinese American with tiki influence.

MAKES 16 pieces
PREP TIME: 10 minutes
COOK TIME: 6 minutes

6 ounces regular
  cream cheese, at
  room temperature

3 ounces canned, fresh, or
  imitation crabmeat

½ teaspoon salt

1 teaspoon toasted
  sesame oil

16 square wonton wrappers

½ cup canola oil

1. In a bowl, mix together the cream cheese, crabmeat, salt, and sesame oil.

2. Place one wrapper on the palm of your hand. Add 1 teaspoon of filling to the center. Dip your finger in water and wet two edges of the wrapper. Fold the wrapper over to form a triangle. Press out the air, then press the edges to seal.

3. In a sauté pan or skillet, pour in the canola oil and heat on high. Reduce the heat to medium, add the rangoon, and cook on each side for 2 minutes, or until golden brown.

4. Transfer to paper towels to drain, then serve.

SERVING TIP: Serve crab rangoon with store-bought sweet and sour sauce or honey mustard. Make your own honey mustard by mixing equal parts yellow mustard, honey, and mayo. Season with a touch of vinegar and salt.

CHICKEN CHOW MEIN, PAGE 39

THREE
Rice and Noodles

Rice and noodles are staples of Asian cuisine. Almost every protein or vegetarian dish you find in this cookbook will be served with either rice or noodles. Unlike American cuisine, where the starch or carb component of a balanced meal can come in different forms—bread, pasta, grains, or even root vegetables—Asian cuisines typically use only rice or noodles. Every menu you see at Asian restaurants will have a whole rice and noodle section, and even if you don't order from that section, the entrée you order will most certainly come with rice. In this chapter, we will cover a wide variety of rice and noodle favorites that have been brought over to the United States.

FUN ASIAN FOOD FACT

The diets of Southern Asians and Northern Asians vary greatly due to differing climates. In Southern Asia, where it can be hot and humid, the diet is heavily based on rice and rice noodles. In Northern Asia, where it's cold and dry, the diet is based on wheat products—mainly dumplings, noodles, steamed buns, stuffed buns, and breads. In Southern Asia, popular Vietnamese dishes include Hanoi Chicken Pho (page 43) and Rice Noodles with Shrimp (page 44), which are rice-based meals. Compare those to Spicy Dandan Noodles (page 40) and Chicken Chow Mein (page 39), which are wheat-based and hail from the northern parts of China.

Chicken Chow Mein

NUT-FREE ❀ FASTER THAN DELIVERY ❀ ONE PAN ❀ TAKEOUT FAVORITE

Every Chinese restaurant has this dish, regardless of what regional cuisine it features. And because of this, the quality and taste of chicken chow mein varies greatly. This version uses store-bought chicken, which makes it faster to prepare, more flavorful, and less oily.

SERVES 4
PREP TIME: 5 minutes
COOK TIME: 8 minutes

1 tablespoon canola oil

2 cups shredded store-bought rotisserie chicken

1 teaspoon minced ginger

1 cup shredded carrots

2 cups shredded cabbage

6 cups cooked soft chow mein noodles

4 cups baby spinach

¼ cup soy sauce

3 tablespoons hoisin sauce

1 tablespoon balsamic vinegar

1 teaspoon cornstarch

1 teaspoon water

1. In a wok or cast-iron skillet, pour in the oil and heat on high. Add the chicken, ginger, carrots, and cabbage and stir-fry for 2 minutes.

2. Add the noodles, spinach, soy sauce, hoisin sauce, and vinegar and stir-fry for 3 minutes.

3. Mix together the cornstarch and water to make a slurry. Add it to the wok and stir-fry for 2 minutes. Serve.

SWAP IT: Substitute the soft chow mein noodles with dried pasta, such as thick spaghetti or bucatini. Cook, drain, and coat it in a touch of oil.

TAKE A SHORTCUT: Buy shredded carrots and cabbage to save on prep time.

Spicy Dandan Noodles

FASTER THAN DELIVERY

The term *dandan* refers to the poles that peddlers use to carry baskets of noodles on their shoulders to sell on the street. This dish originates from the Sichuan Province, which is known for its spices, thus the authentic version of dandan mein would be swimming in chile oil and mouth-numbing Sichuan peppercorns. The Americanized version is sweeter and may have peanut butter or sesame paste incorporated.

SERVES 4
PREP TIME: 5 minutes
COOK TIME: 10 minutes

6 cups water

16 ounces fresh linguine or dried egg pasta

2 tablespoons canola oil

8 ounces ground pork

2 tablespoons dried chile flakes

¼ teaspoon salt

¼ cup soy sauce

2 tablespoons chunky peanut butter

1 tablespoon black vinegar

2 tablespoons sugar

½ cup chopped scallions

1. In a stockpot, bring the water to a boil over high heat. Add the noodles and cook for 2 minutes, or until al dente. Reserve ¼ cup of pasta water, then drain the noodles and set aside.

2. In a wok, pour in the oil and heat on high. Add the pork, chile flakes, and salt and stir-fry for 3 minutes, breaking apart the pork with a spatula.

3. Add the soy sauce, peanut butter, vinegar, sugar, and reserved pasta water and stir-fry for 4 minutes. Be sure to whisk with the spatula to fully incorporate the sauce and break down the peanut butter chunks.

4. Transfer the cooked noodles to serving bowls. Pour the pork sauce over the noodles. Garnish with the scallions and serve.

SERVING TIP: For a more authentic take on this recipe, drizzle Sichuan peppercorn oil and chile oil into the sauce, then garnish with crushed peanuts and Chinese pickled mustard greens.

Egg Spam Macaroni Soup

NUT-FREE ✿ **SOY-FREE** ✿ **5 INGREDIENTS** ✿ **FASTER THAN DELIVERY**

This dish is a staple breakfast item in Hong Kong's *cha chaan teng*. These restaurants specialize in Hong Kong–style Western dishes, which can be attributed to Hong Kong's long history of British influence. Here, locals partake in milk teas, cakes, toasts, spaghetti, macaroni, and more.

SERVES 4
PREP TIME: 5 minutes
COOK TIME: 15 minutes

5 cups store-bought chicken broth

2 cups dried macaroni

2 tablespoons canola oil

4 eggs

¼ teaspoon salt

1 can Spam, cut into 4 pieces

1. In a saucepot, bring the broth to a boil over high heat. Add the macaroni and cook for 10 minutes, or until al dente.

2. Meanwhile, in a large nonstick sauté pan or skillet, pour in the oil and heat on medium. Add the eggs and cook, sunny-side up, for about 5 minutes, or until the whites are set and the yolks are done to your liking. Sprinkle with the salt and set aside.

3. Ladle macaroni and broth into four bowls. Top each bowl with a piece of Spam (the soup will warm it) and an egg and serve.

SERVING TIP: Add frozen peas and carrots to the soup for an Asian twist on chicken noodle soup.

Minced Beef over Rice

NUT-FREE ✿ FASTER THAN DELIVERY

This is a popular comfort food on Cantonese restaurant menus. To make lunch affordable and fast, rice plates with sautéed, braised, or steamed proteins and veggies became popular. This dish is extra tasty when reheated the next day, as the sauce and flavor of the beef gets absorbed into the rice.

SERVES 4
PREP TIME: 5 minutes
COOK TIME: 25 minutes

2 tablespoons canola oil

1 pound ground beef

1 cup frozen peas

2 tablespoons oyster sauce

2 tablespoons soy sauce

2 tablespoons mirin or dry white wine

2 cups store-bought beef stock

1 teaspoon sugar

1 tablespoon freshly ground black pepper

1 teaspoon cornstarch

1 teaspoon water

4 egg yolks

6 cups Steamed Rice (page 19)

1. In a wok, pour in the oil and heat on high. Add the beef, peas, oyster sauce, soy sauce, mirin, stock, sugar, and pepper and stir-fry for 2 minutes, breaking the beef apart with a spatula.

2. Cover the wok and cook for another 5 minutes, stirring occasionally.

3. Mix together the cornstarch and water to make a slurry. Add it to the wok and stir-fry for 1 minute.

4. Divide the rice among four bowls.

5. Add the beef mixture to the bowls, top with a yolk, and serve immediately. To eat, mix the yolk into the beef and rice, which will cook it and create a creamy, rich consistency.

SWAP IT: If raw yolks are not desirable, use poached eggs.

Hanoi Chicken Pho

GLUTEN-FREE ❀ NUT-FREE ❀ TAKEOUT FAVORITE

This recipe was inspired by the famous pho ga at the Turtle Tower restaurant in San Francisco. With a few shortcuts, you can taste this amazing Hanoi-style pho in less than an hour.

SERVES 4
PREP TIME: 15 minutes
COOK TIME: 35 minutes

1 whole store-bought rotisserie chicken

4 quarts store-bought chicken stock

2 tablespoons coriander seeds

3 whole cloves

1 medium yellow onion, quartered

1 (3-inch) piece ginger

½ teaspoon salt

3 tablespoons fish sauce

2 teaspoons sugar

6 cups water

1 (14-ounce) package dried rice noodles

1 cup fresh cilantro leaves

½ cup chopped scallions

3 limes, cut into wedges

1. Separate the chicken meat from the bone, then shred it into small pieces and set aside.

2. In a stockpot, combine the bones and stock and bring to a boil over high heat. Cook for 15 minutes.

3. Meanwhile, combine the coriander and cloves in a small sauté pan or skillet over medium heat and toast for 4 minutes, stirring frequently to prevent burning. Set aside.

4. Add the toasted spices, onion, and ginger to the broth. Reduce the heat to medium and simmer for 15 minutes.

5. Strain out the solids, leaving the broth in the stockpot. Stir in the salt, fish sauce, and sugar.

6. In a separate saucepot, bring the water to a boil over high heat. Add the noodles and cook for 45 seconds, or according to the package directions.

7. Transfer the noodles to serving bowls. Add broth and top with the shredded chicken, cilantro, scallion, and lime. Serve.

Rice Noodles with Shrimp (Bún Chả)

GLUTEN-FREE ❀ NUT-FREE ❀ FASTER THAN DELIVERY

Bún chả is a cold noodle salad topped with proteins—such as grilled pork, chicken, beef, shrimp, or tofu—and served with *nước chấm* (a sweet chile dipping sauce), pickled veggies, and fresh herbs.

SERVES 4
PREP TIME: 10 minutes, plus 1 hour to soak skewers
COOK TIME: 10 minutes

FOR THE SHRIMP AND NOODLES

24 medium shrimp, peeled and deveined

½ teaspoon salt

½ teaspoon sugar

2 tablespoons lime juice

4 cups water

3 cups soaked thin rice noodles (vermicelli)

1 cup fresh mint leaves

1 cup grated carrots

1 cup shredded lettuce

FOR THE NƯỚC CHẤM

1 cup hot water

⅓ cup fish sauce

½ cup sugar

1 teaspoon minced garlic

1 teaspoon dried chile flakes

1. Soak 4 long skewers in water for 1 hour.

2. To make the shrimp and noodles, season the shrimp with the salt, sugar, and lime juice. Thread 6 pieces on each skewer. Grill for 2 minutes on each side. Set aside.

3. In a saucepot, bring the water to a boil over high heat. Add the noodles and cook for 45 seconds. Drain the noodles and rinse them under cold water.

4. Divide the noodles into 4 bowls. Top each with the mint, carrots, lettuce, and a skewer of shrimp.

5. To make the nước chấm, whisk together the water, fish sauce, sugar, garlic, and chile flakes in a bowl. Serve on the side as a dressing.

SWAP IT: Swap out nước chấm for hoisin sauce, soy sauce, and sriracha.

Crab Fried Rice

NUT-FREE ❁ FASTER THAN DELIVERY ❁ ONE POT ❁ TAKEOUT FAVORITE

Seafood is plentiful in Southeast Asia. Thai-style crab fried rice is a popular dish that has been imported into the United States with great success, as both crab and fried rice are well liked by Americans. Fried rice is always best when made with day-old rice.

SERVES 4
PREP TIME: 5 minutes
COOK TIME: 8 minutes

2 tablespoons canola oil, divided

2 eggs, whisked

3 garlic cloves, minced

½ cup chopped scallions

1 teaspoon minced ginger

1 Thai bird's eye chile, minced

3 cups leftover Steamed Rice (page 19)

3 teaspoons fish sauce

2 tablespoons soy sauce

1 (6-ounce) can lump crabmeat

½ teaspoon white pepper or black pepper

1 lime, quartered

1. In a wok, pour in 1 tablespoon of oil and heat on high. Add the eggs and stir-fry for 1 minute. Remove the scrambled eggs from the wok and set aside.

2. Heat the remaining 1 tablespoon of oil in the wok, still over high heat. Add the garlic, scallions, ginger, and chile and stir-fry for 1 minute.

3. Add the rice and stir-fry for 3 minutes, using the flat part of the spatula to press down on the rice and break apart clumps.

4. Add the fish sauce, soy sauce, crab, scrambled egg, and pepper and stir-fry for 2 minutes. Garnish with the lime and serve.

SWAP IT: If crab can't be found, use shrimp.

Drunken Noodles with Chicken (Pad Kee Mao)

NUT-FREE ❁ FASTER THAN DELIVERY ❁ TAKEOUT FAVORITE

Spicy and savory, drunken noodles are a top noodle dish at Thai restaurants in the United States. Legend has it that pad kee mao is called "drunken noodles" because one needs beer to help quench the thirst that comes after eating this famously spicy dish.

SERVES 4
PREP TIME: 15 minutes
COOK TIME: 8 minutes

4 quarts water

14 ounces dried wide rice noodles

2 tablespoons canola oil

1 pound chicken breast, thinly sliced

1 garlic clove, minced

1 cup sliced scallions

3 tablespoons fish sauce

¼ cup oyster sauce

3 tablespoons soy sauce

1 tablespoon sugar

1 teaspoon chile powder

½ cup fresh Thai basil leaves

1. In a stockpot, bring the water to a boil over high heat. Add the noodles and cook for about 5 minutes until al dente, or according to package directions. Drain and set them aside.

2. In a wok, pour in the oil and heat on high. Add the chicken and garlic and stir-fry for 3 minutes.

3. Add the scallions, fish sauce, oyster sauce, soy sauce, sugar, and chile powder and stir-fry for 2 minutes.

4. Add the noodles and Thai basil and stir-fry for 2 minutes. Serve.

SERVING TIPS: To achieve that beautiful dark caramel color of drunken noodles, use 2 teaspoons of dark soy sauce.

Coconut Sticky Rice

**GLUTEN-FREE ❀ NUT-FREE ❀ SOY-FREE ❀ VEGETARIAN
5 INGREDIENTS ❀ FASTER THAN DELIVERY ❀ TAKEOUT FAVORITE**

You can't have Thai food without sticky rice, whether it's used to sop up spicy curries or serve with stir-fried dishes. Now you can make your own at home with the help of a rice cooker.

SERVES 4
PREP TIME: 5 minutes
COOK TIME: 25 minutes

1 cup sweet rice

1 cup jasmine rice

1 (13.5-ounce) can unsweetened, full-fat coconut milk

2 cups water

½ teaspoon salt

¼ cup toasted coconut

1. In a rice cooker, pour in the sweet rice, jasmine rice, coconut milk, water, and salt.

2. Stir and press cook "white rice."

3. Once the rice is done, open the lid and fluff the rice with a fork. Cover for 5 minutes.

4. Garnish with the toasted coconut and serve.

SERVING TIP: To add an extra boost of coconut flavor, cook the rice with shredded coconut and finish the rice with a spoonful of coconut oil.

Chicken Fat Rice

NUT-FREE ✿ FASTER THAN DELIVERY

Chicken Fat Rice is traditionally made with chicken fat, chicken broth, and aromatics such as ginger, pandan leaf, and garlic. The rice not only smells incredible but also tastes amazing even when eaten on its own. To make it easier, butter is used here instead of chicken fat.

SERVES 4
PREP TIME: 5 minutes
COOK TIME: 25 minutes

1 pound chicken bones

1 teaspoon salt

2 cups jasmine rice

3 tablespoons
  unsalted butter

2 garlic cloves, minced

2½ cups store-bought
  chicken stock

2 pandan leaves or
  bay leaves

1. Coat the chicken bones with the salt.

2. Rinse the rice with water until the water runs clear, then set aside.

3. In a saucepot, melt the butter over high heat. Add the garlic and cook for 10 seconds. Add the rice and cook, stirring constantly, for 1 minute.

4. Add the stock, bones, and pandan leaves and bring to a boil. Reduce the heat to low, cover, and simmer for 20 minutes.

5. Remove from the heat and let it sit for 10 minutes. Remove and discard the chicken bones and pandan leaves and serve.

SWAP IT: If you prefer a lighter, healthier substitute, you can try using coconut oil instead of butter.

Shoyu Pork Corn Ramen

NUT-FREE ❀ FASTER THAN DELIVERY ❀ ONE POT ❀ TAKEOUT FAVORITE

In major cities, it seems like a new ramen shop opens every few months. Ramen shops usually feature a special house broth, such as tonkotsu (pork bone), shoyu (soy), or miso. This is a remixed version of shoyu ramen. Traditional shoyu takes time to make, but this shortcut method gives you the same taste in only 15 minutes.

SERVES 4
PREP TIME: 5 minutes
COOK TIME: 10 minutes

6 cups water

4 packages Maruchan beef ramen noodle soup

1 teaspoon sake (optional)

1 cup corn

4 eggs

12 thin slices cooked pork loin

½ cup finely chopped scallions

4 nori sheets (optional)

1. In a stockpot, bring the water to a boil over high heat. Add the noodles and their seasoning packs, sake (if using), and corn and crack the raw eggs into the pot to cook for 3 minutes.

2. Remove from the heat and divide the noodles, corn, and eggs equally into bowls, leaving the broth in the pot.

3. Add the pork loin and cook for 1 minute.

4. Top each bowl with the pork and pour broth over. Garnish with the scallions and nori (if using). Serve.

SWAP IT: Swap pork loin for roast beef to make beef ramen. Pickled ginger, dried chile flakes, and bean sprouts are also great additions.

Beef Bowl (Gyūdon)

NUT-FREE ✿ FASTER THAN DELIVERY ✿ ONE POT

The word *gyūdon* means "beef bowl" in Japanese, and it became wildly popular thanks to Yoshinoya, a large beef-bowl fast-food chain. The dish originated from gyunabe and sukiyaki, in which beef slices are cooked in a pot with sukiyaki sauce and vegetables. The Japanese then started serving it over rice, creating the beef rice bowl.

SERVES 4
PREP TIME: 5 minutes
COOK TIME: 10 minutes

2 pounds shaved beef steak

2 tablespoons toasted sesame oil

2 teaspoons cornstarch

4 tablespoons soy sauce

2 tablespoons mirin or dry white wine

4½ teaspoons sugar, divided

3 tablespoons canola oil

1 small yellow onion, thinly sliced

½ teaspoon salt

3 tablespoons hoisin sauce

6 cups Steamed Rice (page 19)

1. In a bowl, combine the beef, sesame oil, cornstarch, soy sauce, mirin, and 4 teaspoons of sugar and marinate for 5 minutes.

2. Meanwhile, heat the canola oil in a wok over medium heat. Add the onion, salt, and remaining ½ teaspoon of sugar and stir-fry for 3 minutes.

3. Add the beef to the wok and stir-fry for 6 minutes, or until fully cooked. Remove from the heat, add the hoisin sauce, and stir. Serve over the rice.

SERVING TIPS: Add store-bought Kizami *beni shōga*, pickled ginger slices, to the dish for a nice spicy citrus burst.

Japchae

NUT-FREE ✿ VEGETARIAN ✿ FASTER THAN DELIVERY ✿ TAKEOUT FAVORITE

Have fun with japchae and experiment with different veggies such as cabbage, carrots, celery, zucchini, and various colored peppers. Since this noodle has a chewy al dente texture, it holds well even as leftovers, whether you microwave it or eat it cold.

SERVES 4
PREP TIME: 15 minutes
COOK TIME: 10 minutes

6 cups water

8 ounces sweet potato starch noodles (dangmyeon)

1 tablespoon canola oil

1 cup sliced shiitake mushrooms

1 small red bell pepper, thinly sliced

½ teaspoon salt

½ teaspoon white pepper

¼ cup soy sauce

¼ cup ponzu

2 tablespoons sugar

2 cups baby spinach

3 tablespoons toasted sesame oil

1. In a stockpot, bring the water to a boil over high heat. Add the noodles and cook for about 6 minutes, or according to the package directions. Drain the noodles and rinse under cold water. Cut the noodles with scissors to 6 inches in length.

2. In a wok, pour in the canola oil and heat on high. Add the mushrooms and bell pepper and stir-fry for 3 minutes.

3. Reduce the heat to medium. Add the noodles, salt, pepper, soy sauce, ponzu, sugar, spinach, and sesame oil and stir-fry for 5 minutes. Serve.

SWAP IT: If you can't find dangmyeon, use glass noodles (aka cellophane noodles), which are similar and can be found in your grocery's international aisle. If you can't find ponzu, use soy sauce and lemon or lime juice and the zest.

Street Dog Bibimbap

NUT-FREE ✿ FASTER THAN DELIVERY ✿ TAKEOUT FAVORITE

In Los Angeles in particular, Korean American chefs have developed all sorts of Korean American fusion dishes, from adding kimchi to hot dogs and tacos to throwing cheese on Korean stews. Bibimbap, which literally means "mixed rice," incorporates seasoned veggies, pickles, proteins, and more. This version is an ode to the Korean fusion movement.

SERVES 4
PREP TIME: 5 minutes
COOK TIME: 25 minutes

6 cups Steamed Rice
    (page 19)

3 tablespoons canola
    oil, divided

1 cup julienned carrots

4 hot dogs, cut into
    thick slices

1 teaspoon salt

½ teaspoon sugar

3 cups spinach

4 eggs

½ cup store-bought kimchi

Gochujang, for serving

1. Cook the steamed rice using the stovetop or rice cooker method.

2. In a wok, pour in 1 tablespoon of oil and heat on high. Add the carrots, hot dogs, salt, and sugar and stir-fry for 3 minutes. Add the spinach and stir-fry for 2 minutes, until wilted.

3. Divide the rice among 4 bowls and add the vegetable mix on top.

4. In the empty wok, heat the remaining 2 tablespoons of oil. Add the eggs and cook, sunny-side up, for about 5 minutes, or until the whites are set and the yolk is done to your liking.

5. Top each bowl with an egg and garnish with the kimchi.

6. Drizzle with the gochujang and serve.

SWAP IT: Swap out hot dogs for kielbasa or Polish sausages if you like it spicier. Or try bulk sausage, sautéing it before adding it to the rice.

Mie Goreng

NUT-FREE ❀ FASTER THAN DELIVERY ❀ TAKEOUT FAVORITE

Each Asian cuisine has its own version of stir-fried noodles. The Chinese have chow mein, the Japanese have yakisoba, and the Indonesians have mie goreng. The flavors of Indonesian fried noodles are sweeter and spicier than its Asian counterparts, with high usage of ketchup and palm sugar.

SERVES 4
PREP TIME: 15 minutes
COOK TIME: 10 minutes

2 tablespoons canola oil

3 eggs, whisked

2 garlic cloves, minced

2 tablespoons sambal

4 cups cooked chow mein noodles

2 whole tomatoes, sliced

4 tablespoons ketchup

1 tablespoon dark or regular soy sauce

1 tablespoon sugar

1 lime, quartered

1. In a wok, pour in the oil and heat on high. Add the eggs, garlic, and sambal and stir-fry for 1 minute.

2. Add the noodles, tomatoes, ketchup, soy sauce, and sugar and stir-fry for 5 minutes, or until the noodles absorb the sauce and are fragrant.

3. Divide the noodles among plates and serve with a wedge of lime for squeezing.

INGREDIENT TIP: Sambal is an Indonesian chile paste made with shrimp paste, garlic, ginger, shallots, sugar, and lime juice. Find it in the Asian section of the grocery store or online.

SWAP IT: Swap sambal for red curry paste, which has similar flavors. Add extra sugar and a touch of fish sauce to balance the flavors out.

Pad Thai with Tofu

FASTER THAN DELIVERY ✿ TAKEOUT FAVORITE

Pad Thai was created in the 1930s by the prime minister of Thailand to evoke a greater sense of Thai nationalism and pride. This sweet, tangy, and slightly spicy stir-fried rice noodle dish is the gateway to Thai cuisine in America, not to mention listed on a CNN list of the world's 50 best foods to eat.

SERVES 4
PREP TIME: 30 minutes
COOK TIME: 10 minutes

8 ounces dry pad Thai rice noodles

2 tablespoons canola oil

1 (9-ounce) package braised firm tofu, cut into chunks

2 eggs

4 tablespoons fish sauce

4 tablespoons sugar

1 tablespoon ketchup

2 tablespoons rice wine vinegar or lime juice

1 tablespoon sriracha

5 ounces bean sprouts

¼ cup crushed roasted peanuts

1. In a large bowl, soak the noodles in lukewarm water for 30 minutes, then drain.

2. In a wok, pour in the oil and heat on high. Add the soaked noodles and tofu and stir-fry for 2 minutes.

3. Move the noodles and tofu to one side of the wok and add the eggs, scrambling for 30 seconds. Add the fish sauce, sugar, ketchup, vinegar, and sriracha and stir-fry for 2 minutes.

4. Add half of the bean sprouts and peanuts and stir-fry for 2 more minutes.

5. Garnish with the rest of the nuts and bean sprouts and serve.

INGREDIENT TIP: Buy whole dry-roasted peanuts and crush them on a cutting board, using the back of a pan to push down on the nuts. Add shrimp or chicken to the pad Thai to make it heartier.

THAI COCONUT SOUP (TOM KHA GAI), PAGE 67

FOUR
Soups, Stews, and Curries

Though cuisines can differ greatly in the various regions of each Asian country, one thing is true: Variations of soups, stews, and curries have become an important part of day-to-day diets. In many instances, they serve a purpose. In Korea, soups such as galbitang are eaten to fight off the freezing temperatures. In Southeast Asian countries, where the climate is hotter, various spices are used to make spicy soups such as laksa in Malaysia, which promotes sweating that helps cool down the body. In this chapter, you will learn how to make signature curry, stew, and soup dishes.

FUN ASIAN FOOD FACT

Did you know that the British traders in the 19th century made curry popular in China, Thailand, Japan, and other Asian countries? The Portuguese were the first to bring back spices such as black pepper, cardamom, and cloves, a valuable trade commodity. Lacking a word to describe these spices used to create thickened delicious stews, they invented their own and called it *carel*, taken from *kari*, a word that means "sauce laced with spices" in Tamil, a language spoken in India. The British East India Company took over the spice trade from the Portuguese and pronounced the word *carel* as "curry." The British manufactured curry powder mix in India and spread it throughout Asia via trade. While countries in Asia, such as Thailand, have their own curries, they also adopted the Western yellow curry powder version. Popular curry dishes such as Massaman Beef Curry (page 68) fused new spices with Thai ingredients. The Japanese took the mix and cooked it with fruit and vegetables to make savory-sweet stews and sauces, all to be enjoyed over rice.

Egg Flower Soup (Dàn Huā Tāng)

**GLUTEN-FREE ❊ NUT-FREE ❊ SOY-FREE ❊ 5 INGREDIENTS
FASTER THAN DELIVERY ❊ ONE POT ❊ TAKEOUT FAVORITE**

The name of this dish comes from the fact that the egg spreads out like a flower when it's poured into hot broth and cooks into beautiful ribbons. The Americanized version uses cornstarch to thicken the soup. The traditional version is not thickened.

SERVES 4
PREP TIME: 2 minutes
COOK TIME: 5 minutes

4 cups store-bought chicken broth

3 eggs, whisked

Salt

2 teaspoons toasted sesame oil

¼ cup minced scallions

1. In a stockpot, bring the broth to a boil over high heat.

2. In a circular motion, slowly pour the eggs into the broth, stirring until the resulting ribbons are distributed evenly. Let it boil for 1 minute. Taste and season with salt as needed.

3. Pour the soup into bowls. Drizzle each with the oil, garnish with the scallions, and serve.

SERVING TIPS: Be creative by adding veggies such as corn, sliced mushrooms, frozen chopped spinach, kale, or diced soft tofu.

Chicken Corn Soup

GLUTEN-FREE ✿ NUT-FREE ✿ SOY-FREE
FASTER THAN DELIVERY ✿ ONE POT

This dish is a delicious combination of two things we love: sweet creamed corn soup and savory egg flower soup simmered with chicken. Chinese immigrants took a very American dish and fused it with Chinese flavors, turning it into a quintessential Chinese American comfort food served across the United States.

SERVES 4
PREP TIME: 5 minutes
COOK TIME: 8 minutes

5 cups store-bought chicken broth

1 cup ground chicken breast

1 (15-ounce) can creamed sweet corn

1 (15-ounce) can corn

½ teaspoon salt

1 egg, whisked

1 tablespoon cornstarch

1 tablespoon water

1. In a stockpot, bring the broth to a boil over high heat.

2. Add the chicken and whisk to break it apart, then boil for 3 minutes.

3. Add the creamed corn and corn and boil for 2 minutes. Add the salt.

4. In a circular motion, slowly pour the egg into the broth, stirring until the resulting ribbons are distributed evenly.

5. Mix together the cornstarch and water to make a slurry. Add it to the soup and stir vigorously for 1 minute, until thickened. Serve.

SWAP IT: For a vegetarian-friendly version, omit the chicken and swap out chicken broth for vegetable broth.

Wonton Soup

NUT-FREE ❁ 5 INGREDIENTS ❁ FASTER THAN DELIVERY TAKEOUT FAVORITE

The history of wontons is long and the varieties available in China alone are vast. One could dedicate an entire book to the subject. This version combines Cantonese, Shanghainese, and Western influences. The skin is thin like Cantonese wontons, the filling is Western, and the broth is Shanghainese.

SERVES 4
PREP TIME: 15 minutes
COOK TIME: 8 minutes

5 cups store-bought chicken broth

4 thin slices ginger

20 uncooked pork wontons (see Red Oil Tossed Pork Wontons, page 25)

White pepper or freshly ground black pepper

2 tablespoons soy sauce

½ cup cilantro leaves

1. In a stockpot, bring the broth to a boil over high heat. Add the ginger and wontons and cook until they float, about 5 minutes.

2. Season to taste with pepper and stir in the soy sauce.

3. Ladle the broth and wontons into bowls. Garnish with the cilantro and serve.

TAKE A SHORTCUT: To make wonton soup even faster, use store-bought frozen wontons or dumplings instead of wrapping your own.

Korean Short Rib Soup (Galbitang)

GLUTEN-FREE ❀ **NUT-FREE** ❀ **SOY-FREE** ❀ **5 INGREDIENTS** ❀ **ONE POT**

Galbitang is the perfect comfort meal during the winter, and it can be enjoyed in different ways: Add rice to make a porridge, add noodles to make noodle soup, or serve alongside a bowl of rice and some kimchi.

SERVES 4
PREP TIME: 30 minutes
COOK TIME: 4 hours

6 pounds Korean-style short ribs

4 thick slices ginger

1 large radish, peeled and cut into 1-inch-thick slices

1 large yellow onion, quartered

1 tablespoon salt

1 tablespoon freshly ground black pepper

½ cup chopped scallions

1. In a stockpot, place the ribs and pour in enough water to cover the ribs by 1½ inches. Soak for 30 minutes to purge impurities and blood. Strain and rinse the ribs, then scrub the pot clean.

2. Place the ribs back into the pot, add fresh water to cover, and bring to a boil over high heat. Boil for 2 minutes, then discard the water and rinse the ribs again.

3. Place the ribs back into the pot and add the ginger. Add fresh water to cover by 1½ inches. Bring to a boil over high heat, then reduce the heat to medium-low and simmer, covered, for 3 hours.

4. Add the radish and onion and simmer for 1 more hour.

5. Season with the salt and pepper, garnish with the scallions, and serve.

INGREDIENT TIP: Korean-style short ribs are cut across the bone into thin strips. The cut is available at most Asian groceries, or ask your butcher to cut the ribs "flanken style" to order.

Kimchi Army Stew (Budae Jjigae)

NUT-FREE ❀ FASTER THAN DELIVERY ❀ ONE POT

This dish is something you can throw together in a pinch. Korean army stew was created after the Korean War ended. As food became scarce, Koreans used the surplus processed meats left by the Americans to cook with, which introduced Western processed meats to Korean American cuisine.

SERVES 4
PREP TIME: 15 minutes
COOK TIME: 10 minutes

2 cups store-bought kimchi

6 cups store-bought beef broth

3 hot dogs, sliced

1 can Spam, sliced

½ cup chopped scallions

1 large carrot, thinly sliced

1 tablespoon gochujang

1 tablespoon Korean chile powder (gochugaru)

2 (3-ounce) packages Maruchan dried ramen noodles

1. In a Dutch oven, combine the kimchi, broth, hot dogs, Spam, scallions, carrot, gochujang, and chile powder over high heat and bring to a boil. Cook for 5 minutes.

2. Add the ramen noodles and cook for 3 minutes, or until the noodles are tender, and serve.

TIPS: Add tofu or other veggies to make the stew heartier. A slice of processed cheddar cheese such as Kraft Singles can be added on top to create a cheesy, rich consistency to the stew.

Sinigang

NUT-FREE ✿ ONE POT ✿ TAKEOUT FAVORITE

Sinigang is a very popular dish for Filipino families. It's prepared on special occasions such as birthdays and when people are feeling under the weather. This sour-and-savory stew is filling yet light and flavorful at the same time, which explains why it's a household favorite.

SERVES 4
PREP TIME: 10 minutes
COOK TIME: 1 hour

1 tablespoon canola oil

2 pounds pork belly, cut into 1-inch-thick slices

2 tablespoons fish sauce

1 medium yellow onion, quartered

2 medium tomatoes, quartered

6 cups store-bought beef broth

8 okra pods

1 tablespoon tamarind paste

Salt

1. In a stockpot, pour in the oil and heat on high. Add the pork, fish sauce, and onion and stir-fry for 3 minutes.

2. Add the tomatoes and broth and bring to a boil. Boil for 2 minutes, then reduce the heat to medium and simmer, covered, for 45 minutes.

3. Add the okra and tamarind paste. Increase the heat to high and bring back to a boil. Cook for 5 minutes, or until the okra are tender.

4. Taste and season with salt as needed. Serve.

SWAP IT: Sinigang is flexible. Swap the pork belly with pork ribs, beef, chicken, or seafood. Swap okra with eggplant, green beans, potato, taro, or spinach—whatever is available and in season.

Chicken Kare Kare

GLUTEN-FREE ✿ ONE POT ✿ TAKEOUT FAVORITE

Traditionally, kare kare uses eggplant, long beans, and bok choy. This simplified version uses only bok choy, which brings down prep time but still tastes great. Annatto imparts the traditional orange hue to the stew, but it's optional as it doesn't add much distinctive flavor.

SERVES 4
PREP TIME: 10 minutes
COOK TIME: 45 minutes

3 tablespoons canola oil

2 pounds boneless chicken thighs, cubed

3 garlic cloves, chopped

1 tablespoon fish sauce

3 cups store-bought chicken broth

2 cups coarsely chopped bok choy

½ cup peanut butter (sweetened)

1 tablespoon cornstarch

1 tablespoon water

1 teaspoon salt

1 teaspoon annatto powder (optional)

1. In a Dutch oven, pour in the oil and heat on high. Add the chicken, garlic, and fish sauce and stir-fry for 3 minutes.

2. Add the broth and bring to a boil. Reduce the heat to low and simmer, covered, for 30 minutes.

3. Add the bok choy and peanut butter, stirring until smooth. Cook for 5 minutes, or until the boy choy is tender.

4. Mix together the cornstarch and water to make a slurry. Add it to the stew and stir vigorously for 1 minute to thicken. Season with the salt.

5. Whisk together the annatto powder (if using) with a bit of hot water. Add it to the stew and cook for 2 minutes. Serve.

SWAP IT: Swap bok choy for kale.

Myanmarese Fish Chowder (Mohinga)

GLUTEN-FREE ❁ NUT-FREE ❁ SOY-FREE
FASTER THAN DELIVERY ❁ ONE POT ❁ TAKEOUT FAVORITE

This Southern Myanmarese chowder is recognized by many as a national dish. It's usually eaten as breakfast and can be topped with split pea crackers, rice noodles, eggs, broad bean fritters, onions, cilantro, and lime wedges. Traditionally, toasted rice powder is used to thicken the soup. To make this dish more approachable, the ingredients have been pared down, but the flavors and textures have not.

SERVES 4
PREP TIME: 15 minutes
COOK TIME: 10 minutes

1 tablespoon canola oil

1 teaspoon turmeric

3 shallots, peeled and quartered

3 large slices ginger

4 cups store-bought vegetable broth

6 catfish fillets, cut into 2-inch chunks

4 bay leaves

2 tablespoons fish sauce

½ teaspoon chile powder

1 teaspoon salt

1 cup lentil chips

3 lemongrass stalks, peeled and smashed

1. In a Dutch oven, pour in the oil and heat on high. Add the turmeric, shallots, and ginger and stir-fry for 2 minutes.

2. Add the broth and bring to a boil. Reduce the heat to medium. Add the fish, bay leaves, fish sauce, and chile powder and simmer for 8 minutes, or until the fish is cooked through.

3. Season with the salt. Stir vigorously to break apart the fish.

4. Divide the soup among bowls. Garnish with the lentil chips and lemongrass and serve.

SWAP IT: Lemongrass is traditionally used in this soup, but swap with the juice of 1 lime and its zest instead.

Thai Coconut Soup (Tom Kha Gai)

**GLUTEN-FREE ❀ NUT-FREE ❀ SOY-FREE
FASTER THAN DELIVERY ❀ ONE POT ❀ TAKEOUT FAVORITE**

The phrase *tom kha gai* translates to "chicken galangal soup." Galangal looks like ginger, but the flavor is more citrusy and piney. The flesh is harder and cannot be grated, so it must be sliced. Ginger is a fine substitute, though. The flavors in this soup hit all the notes you would expect in Thai food: sweet, spicy, and sour.

**SERVES 4
PREP TIME:** 10 minutes
COOK TIME: 12 minutes

1 teaspoon coconut oil

1 medium shallot,
   thinly sliced

4 cups full-fat coconut milk

2 cups store-bought
   chicken broth

4 thin slices galangal
   or ginger

6 makrut lime leaves

4 chicken tenders,
   thinly sliced

1 cup thinly sliced white
   button mushrooms

1 stalk
   lemongrass, smashed

1 tablespoon fish sauce

½ teaspoon salt

1 tablespoon sugar

½ cup chopped
   fresh cilantro

1. In a Dutch oven, pour in the oil and heat on high. Add the shallot and stir-fry for 1 minute.

2. Add the coconut milk and broth and bring to a boil.

3. Reduce the heat to medium, add the galangal, lime leaves, chicken, mushrooms, lemongrass, fish sauce, salt, and sugar and simmer for 10 minutes, or until the chicken is cooked through.

4. Divide among serving bowls, garnish with the cilantro, and serve.

SWAP IT: Swap the makrut lime leaves for a regular lime's zest and juice. Swap fresh lemongrass with a dehydrated or paste version.

Massaman Beef Curry

GLUTEN-FREE ❁ NUT-FREE ❁ SOY-FREE ❁ ONE POT

Massaman curry, or "curry of the Muslim," was a popular dish among the Muslim community in Siam. The Arabian version used raisins, peanuts, and almonds. The Thai version uses tamarind, lemongrass, and shrimp paste. Simply throw everything in one pot and let it do its magic.

SERVES 4
PREP TIME: 10 minutes
COOK TIME: 2 hours

1½ pounds boneless beef short ribs, cut into 2-inch chunks

2½ cups store-bought beef stock

3 cloves

5 cardamom seeds

2 tablespoons tamarind paste

1 (13.5-ounce) can full-fat coconut milk

1 tablespoon sugar

2 tablespoons Thai red curry paste

2 tablespoons fish sauce

2 russet potatoes, peeled and quartered

4 shallots, peeled

Salt

1. In a stockpot over high heat, combine the beef, stock, cloves, cardamom, and tamarind. Bring to a boil, then reduce the heat to medium and simmer, covered, for 1½ hours.

2. Remove the beef and strain out the spices, but keep the broth in the pot.

3. Whisk in the coconut milk, sugar, curry paste, and fish sauce and bring to a boil. Add the beef, potatoes, and shallots and simmer, uncovered and still over medium heat, for 30 minutes, or until the vegetables are tender.

4. Taste and season with salt as needed. Serve.

INGREDIENT TIP: Add raisins or pineapple to make a sweeter curry.

Miso Soup

NUT-FREE ❧ VEGETARIAN ❧ 5 INGREDIENTS ❧ FASTER THAN DELIVERY
ONE POT ❧ TAKEOUT FAVORITE

Miso soup is the most popular soup in Japanese cuisine. It comes with set meals or sometimes for free before you begin a meal. In Japan, miso soup can be an art form, as chefs experiment with versions made with clams, mushrooms, or even pork fat. This version is an ode to the classic miso soup that Americans have grown to love.

SERVES 4
PREP TIME: 5 minutes
COOK TIME: 5 minutes

4 cups water

¼ cup dried
   wakame (seaweed)

2 tablespoons red or
   white miso

8 ounces soft tofu, cut into
   ½-inch dice

¼ cup sliced scallions

1. In a stockpot, combine the water and wakame and bring to a boil over high heat.

2. Whisk in the miso. Add the tofu and boil for 2 minutes.

3. Divide the soup among bowls, garnish with the scallions, and serve.

INGREDIENT TIP: For a richer miso taste, add dashi powder or bonito flakes. Dashi is a stock base made from kombu and usually fermented fish. It adds umami to broths and sauces.

Chicken Katsu Curry

NUT-FREE ❀ SOY-FREE ❀ 5 INGREDIENTS
FASTER THAN DELIVERY ❀ TAKEOUT FAVORITE

The word *katsu* means "cutlet," and this dish marries two things Americans love: fried chicken and curry. Instead of soft cubes of chicken, this one uses crispy chicken with panko, Japanese bread crumbs. Food trucks dedicated to making katsu curry can now be found in major cities in America.

SERVES 4
PREP TIME: 10 minutes
COOK TIME: 15 minutes

4 chicken breast
    cutlets, pounded

Salt

4 cubes S&B Golden
    Curry Sauce

3 cups water

½ cup all-purpose flour

3 eggs, whisked

1½ cups panko
    bread crumbs

Canola oil, for frying

1. Season the chicken all over with salt and set aside while you start the curry.

2. In a saucepan, put in the curry cubes and heat on high. Slowly whisk in the water until incorporated and a thick sauce forms. Reduce the heat to medium and cook, stirring constantly, for 2 minutes. Remove from the heat.

3. Put the flour, egg, and panko in 3 separate bowls. Dredge the chicken first in the flour, then dip it in the egg, and lastly coat it in panko. Set aside.

4. In a large cast-iron skillet, pour in ¼ inch of oil and heat on high. Add the chicken and shallow-fry for 3 minutes on each side, or until golden brown and cooked through.

5. Transfer the chicken to plates and drizzle the curry sauce on top. Serve.

SERVING TIP: Serve this curry with rice, pickles, and shaved cabbage for a full traditional Japanese meal.

Cambodian Pork Curry

GLUTEN-FREE ❀ NUT-FREE ❀ FASTER THAN DELIVERY ❀ ONE POT

Cambodian curries are less spicy and sweet than Thai curries. Cambodian flavors tend to have a tangy twist due to the use of pickled vegetables. Unlike most Southeast Asian curries, which incorporate some sugar to balance out salty or tart flavors, this curry does not. To get a more authentic flavor, add lime zest and juice at the end.

SERVES 4
PREP TIME: 10 minutes
COOK TIME: 15 minutes

1 tablespoon canola oil

6 shallots, minced

1 red bell pepper, chopped

2 tablespoons yellow curry paste

½ cup pineapple chunks

1 tablespoon tamarind paste

1 (13.5-ounce) can full-fat coconut milk

1½ pounds pork tenderloin, thinly sliced

Salt

1. In a wok, pour in the oil and heat on high. Add the shallots, bell pepper, curry paste, and pineapple and stir-fry for 3 minutes.

2. Stir in the tamarind paste and coconut milk and bring to a boil. Cook for 5 minutes.

3. Add the pork tenderloin, reduce the heat to medium, and simmer for 5 minutes, or until cooked through.

4. Taste and season with salt as needed. Serve.

INGREDIENT TIP: To make this spicy, add fresh Thai bird's eye chiles to it.

Vietnamese Beef Stew (Bò Kho)

NUT-FREE ✿ ONE POT

This hearty, flavorful tomato-based stew can be paired with rice noodles, egg noodles, or a baguette. Serve this version with baguettes and allow your guests to dip the bread into the rich broth for a delicious bite.

SERVES 4
PREP TIME: 15 minutes
COOK TIME: 1 hour

2 stalks lemongrass

2 tablespoons canola oil

1 medium yellow onion, sliced

3 pounds boneless beef short ribs, cut into 2-inch chunks

4 tablespoons tomato paste

2 star anise

8 cups store-bought beef broth

2 cups coconut water

1 tablespoon paprika

2 large carrots, cut into 2-inch-thick slices

3 tablespoons soy sauce

3 tablespoons chile oil

1. Remove and discard the tough, woody part of the lemongrass, then mince the tender parts.

2. In a Dutch oven, pour in the canola oil and heat on high. Add the lemongrass and stir-fry for a few seconds to release its fragrance. Add the onion and beef and stir-fry for 3 minutes.

3. Add the tomato paste, star anise, broth, coconut water, paprika, and carrots and bring to a boil. Reduce the heat to medium-low and simmer, covered, for 1 hour, until everything is tender.

4. Stir in the soy sauce and chile oil and serve.

> **SERVING TIP:** To achieve the bright red color typical of this stew, add annatto powder soaked in water. Serve this dish with traditional toppings, such as sliced raw white onions, Thai basil, and lime wedges.

Malaysian Lamb Rendang

GLUTEN-FREE ✿ SOY-FREE ✿ TAKEOUT FAVORITE

Rendang is an iconic dish for Malaysia, prepared with beef or lamb. It is not to be confused with curries because it has far less liquid and the flavors are more concentrated. Candlenuts are traditionally used to prepare rendang but because they're hard to find, macadamia nuts can be used instead.

SERVES 4
PREP TIME: 15 minutes
COOK TIME: 2½ hours

6 candlenuts or macadamia nuts

1 tablespoon coriander seeds

1 teaspoon turmeric

6 garlic cloves

3 stalks lemongrass, minced

1 (13.5-ounce) can full-fat coconut milk

1 teaspoon salt

1 teaspoon freshly ground black pepper

2 tablespoons canola oil

2 pounds leg of lamb, butterflied

1. Preheat the oven to 325°F.

2. In a food processor, put the candlenuts, coriander, turmeric, garlic, lemongrass, and coconut milk. Blend until smooth. Season with the salt and pepper.

3. In a Dutch oven, pour in the oil and heat on high. Add the lamb and sear on each side for 5 minutes. Pour the marinade over the lamb. Boil for 1 minute.

4. Remove from the heat, cover the pot with foil, and place in the oven. Roast for 2 hours, or until the lamb is fork-tender and the liquid has evaporated.

5. Remove from the oven and let rest for 10 minutes before slicing.

TAKE A SHORTCUT: To cut cooking time, use lamb chops. Use the same method, except sear on both sides on high for 2 minutes and then bake at 400°F for only 10 minutes. Let it rest before serving.

Laksa Soup

GLUTEN-FREE ❁ NUT-FREE ❁ FASTER THAN DELIVERY ❁ TAKEOUT FAVORITE

Laksa is traditionally served with wheat noodles or vermicelli noodles and can come with a variety of toppings, such as fish balls, chicken, tofu puffs, bean sprouts, and fresh herbs. Laksa is found in Malaysia, Singapore, and Indonesia but can vary in style. Regardless of what type, laksa is a pungent soup that will awaken your taste buds.

SERVES 4
PREP TIME: 5 minutes
COOK TIME: 12 minutes

2 tablespoons canola oil

1 (7-ounce) jar laksa paste

6 cups store-bought chicken broth

4 makrut lime leaves or zest and juice of 2 limes

½ teaspoon salt

1 tablespoon brown sugar

12 large prawns, shell on

8 clams

1 (13.5-ounce) can full-fat coconut milk

½ tablespoon fish sauce

½ cup fresh cilantro leaves

1. In a stockpot, pour in the oil and heat on high. Add the laksa paste and stir-fry for 1 minute.

2. Stir in the broth, lime leaves, salt, and sugar and boil for 3 minutes. Add the prawns and clams and boil for 5 minutes.

3. Reduce the heat to medium. Add the coconut milk and simmer for 2 minutes. Remove from the heat and stir in the fish sauce.

4. Garnish with the cilantro and serve.

INGREDIENT TIP: Find laksa paste in the international aisle or online. I recommend the Por Kwan brand as the best. Add turmeric powder or tamarind to make different versions of laksa.

CARAMELIZED BRUSSELS SPROUTS, PAGE 90

FIVE
Vegetables and Tofu

The preparation of vegetables and tofu tends to get a lot of attention and care in Asian countries, especially in China. Based on the vegetable, different seasonings are used to help bring the natural flavor of the ingredient to the forefront. There is also an abundance of tofu products in Asia, many of which we have never even heard of here in the United States. Tofu—soy milk that has been coagulated and pressed into blocks—has been eaten in China for more than 2,000 years. This chapter will introduce you to Asian vegetable cooking. We will teach you to prepare medium-firm tofu and silken tofu and help you master different ways to cook Western and Asian vegetable varieties that are becoming popular in the produce section of average groceries. Now you can tackle vegetables with a whole arsenal of new spices and seasonings that will make vegetable and tofu dishes the highlight of your meal.

FUN ASIAN FOOD FACT

Vegetables are an integral part of the Asian diet. It is said that Asians eat twice as many vegetables as their Western counterparts. What we like to call the "farm-to-table trend," eating only seasonal ingredients, is everyday life in Asia. Rather than the occasional farmers' market, most Asian countries have wet markets, which are open every single day and offer seasonal vegetables, herbs, fruits, seafood, and even livestock. With so many fresh vegetables on hand, it's no wonder that canned or frozen vegetables are not used in traditional Asian cooking. When Asians immigrated to the United States, they started using canned or frozen vegetables and fruits, since they had limited access to fresh vegetables in general, let alone the regional ingredients of their homeland. That's how Western vegetables, such as broccoli, green beans, corn, potatoes, tomatoes, carrots, and celery, made their way into Asian American dishes.

Cold Tofu with Scallions

GLUTEN-FREE ❀ NUT-FREE ❀ VEGETARIAN ❀ 5 INGREDIENTS
FASTER THAN DELIVERY ❀ ONE POT

Tofu was originally introduced in Japan by Buddhist monks from China in the late 8th century. Since most Buddhist monks were vegetarian, tofu was an important source of protein. A book on preparing tofu 100 ways was found dating back to the Edo Period (1600). Tofu in Japanese American cuisine is most commonly served fried in miso soup or ramen, or cold in a salad. This recipe is an incredibly easy way to prepare cold tofu salad using some traditional Zen elements of Japanese cuisine.

SERVES 4 as a side
PREP TIME: 5 minutes

1 (16-ounce) pack soft tofu

½ cup minced scallions

¼ cup ponzu

3 tablespoons toasted
    sesame oil

1. In a shallow bowl, place the block of tofu by flipping the pack upside down into the bowl.

2. Using a knife, slice the tofu vertically, starting from one end and working your way to the other, keeping a ½-inch distance from each slice.

3. Top the tofu with the scallions, drizzle with the ponzu and oil, and serve.

> **INGREDIENT TIP:** Ponzu is a citrus-based soy sauce made from mirin, dried tuna, seaweed, and yuzu. It tastes a bit like soy sauce, but it's milder and has hints of citrus and more umami. Swap with soy sauce and lemon or lime juice and the zest.

Sesame Spinach (Gomae)

**GLUTEN-FREE ❁ NUT-FREE ❁ SOY-FREE ❁ VEGETARIAN
5 INGREDIENTS ❁ FASTER THAN DELIVERY**

This is a cold spinach salad tossed with a rich sesame dressing. This version has a fun visual twist. Instead of mixing spinach with dressing and serving it in a bowl, the spinach is formed into tiny little balls. They sit in a pool of dressing, looking like round green bushes sitting in sand. Allow guests to serve themselves and drizzle the sauce on their spinach.

SERVES 4 as a side
PREP TIME: 10 minutes
COOK TIME: 5 minutes

9 cups spinach with stems (about 3 bunches)

½ cup roasted sesame dressing, such as Kewpie

¼ cup sesame seeds

1. Make an ice bath by filling a large bowl with ice and water. Bring a stockpot of water to a boil over high heat.

2. Cut the spinach bunches in half crosswise, separating the leaves from the stems. Discard the stems and wash the leaves thoroughly.

3. Transfer the spinach to the stockpot and boil for 30 seconds. Plunge the spinach immediately into the ice bath. Drain and squeeze the spinach dry.

4. Pour the dressing into a shallow bowl. Using your hands, form the spinach into golf ball–size balls, place them on top of the dressing, and garnish the spinach with sesame seeds. Serve.

INGREDIENT TIP: Buy fully grown spinach with stems, as it provides better texture than baby spinach when blanched. Roasted sesame dressing is available at most grocery stores; it's great to have around for salads and cold sesame noodles.

Salt and Pepper Edamame

GLUTEN-FREE ❁ NUT-FREE ❁ VEGETARIAN ❁ 5 INGREDIENTS
FASTER THAN DELIVERY ❁ TAKEOUT FAVORITE

Thanks to Japanese American cuisine, edamame has become one of the most commonly ordered appetizers at Asian restaurants. It's a simple, healthy dish that Americans love to nosh on before beginning their meal. It's great with beer, sake, or cocktails and easy to eat. Now you can make your own, as frozen edamame in shells are readily available at grocery stores.

SERVES 4 as a side
PREP TIME: 2 minutes
COOK TIME: 5 minutes

3 teaspoons sea salt or kosher salt, divided

1 (12-ounce) bag frozen edamame

2 teaspoons freshly ground black pepper

1. Bring a stockpot of water to a boil over high heat. Add 1 teaspoon of salt and the edamame. Cook for 5 minutes, or until tender.

2. Drain the edamame and transfer to a bowl. Season with the remaining 2 teaspoons of salt and the pepper. Serve.

SERVING TIP: Edamame is also great cold. Run it under cold water after boiling. Place it in the refrigerator until you need it. Season with salt and pepper right before serving. You can also toss the hot version with butter and honey for a tasty twist.

Garlic Bok Choy

**GLUTEN-FREE ✿ NUT-FREE ✿ SOY-FREE ✿ VEGETARIAN
5 INGREDIENTS ✿ FASTER THAN DELIVERY ✿ ONE POT**

Bok choy is a Chinese cabbage that has become extremely popular in Chinese American cuisine. It's the most popular Chinese vegetable that Americans know of, with maybe Chinese broccoli being second. This fresh take not only tastes better than the restaurant version, but it's also a lot easier to make.

SERVES 4 as a side
PREP TIME: 2 minutes
COOK TIME: 5 minutes

1 tablespoon canola oil

5 garlic cloves, thinly sliced

4 cups water

2 teaspoons salt

1 teaspoon sugar

1 pound bok choy, rinsed
    and drained well

1. In a stockpot, pour in the oil and heat on high. Add the garlic and stir-fry until light brown.

2. Pour in the water and bring to a boil. Add the salt, sugar, and bok choy and boil for 3 minutes.

3. Drain the boy choy and serve.

SERVING TIP: Most Asian vegetable dishes are stir-fried in a wok. However, the heat of the wok is never hot enough in a home kitchen to produce perfectly cooked veggies, which are slightly crisp, bright green, and not soggy. This method prevents soggy, overcooked veggies.

Firecracker Corn

GLUTEN-FREE ❀ **NUT-FREE** ❀ **VEGETARIAN** ❀ **5 INGREDIENTS**
FASTER THAN DELIVERY ❀ **ONE POT**

Firecracker corn started appearing at Asian fusion restaurants more than 20 years ago. Americans' love for corn, fused with some Asian flavors, created a hit. Wok-tossing corn with butter, dried chile flakes, scallions, and a touch of soy makes for a delicious twist on the traditional corn dish.

SERVES 4 as a side
PREP TIME: 2 minutes
COOK TIME: 5 minutes

2 tablespoons
    unsalted butter

2 (15-ounce) cans
    corn, drained

½ teaspoon dried
    chile flakes

½ teaspoon salt

1 teaspoon soy sauce

In a nonstick pan, melt the butter over high heat. Add the corn, chile flakes, salt, and soy sauce and stir-fry for 4 minutes, until tender, and serve.

SERVING TIP: Add minced garlic and minced scallions for more flavor. When corn is in season, use fresh corn off the cob. It takes a little more time, but it's well worth it.

Cumin-Spiced Potato

**GLUTEN-FREE ❀ NUT-FREE ❀ SOY-FREE ❀ VEGETARIAN
5 INGREDIENTS ❀ FASTER THAN DELIVERY**

In Northeastern China, the cuisine is influenced by Russia and Mongolia. Cumin, potato, wheat, corn, cabbage, lamb, and mutton are some ingredients commonly used in this region, unlike Southern China where produce and seafood are plentiful. This dish is inspired by the northeastern region of China and makes for a great spicy potato side dish that Americans can enjoy.

SERVES 4 as a side
PREP TIME: 20 minutes
COOK TIME: 5 minutes

3 russet potatoes, peeled and cut into 1-inch cubes

4 tablespoons canola oil

3 teaspoons cumin powder

2 teaspoons turmeric powder

¼ cup chopped fresh cilantro

2 teaspoons salt

1. In a stockpot, put in the potatoes, add water to cover, and bring to a boil. Cook for 15 minutes, or until the potatoes are tender. Drain them and set aside.

2. In a wok, pour in the oil and heat on medium. Add the cumin and turmeric powder and stir-fry for 30 seconds.

3. Add the potatoes, cilantro, and salt and stir-fry for 2 minutes, making sure to evenly coat the potatoes with spices. Serve.

SERVING TIP: For a more decadent dish, add 1 tablespoon of butter at the end to finish, then add a squeeze of lemon juice. Pair it with roasted chicken to make an East-meets-West meat-and-potatoes dinner.

Dry-Braised Green Beans with Mushrooms

GLUTEN-FREE ❀ NUT-FREE ❀ VEGETARIAN ❀ 5 INGREDIENTS
FASTER THAN DELIVERY ❀ ONE POT ❀ TAKEOUT FAVORITE

This is one of the most popular vegetable dishes you can get at Chinese restaurants. It's usually prepared with either soy sauce, broad bean paste, or fermented black beans and enhanced with aromatics like ginger and garlic. This simple version cuts down cooking time, ingredients, and oil, as we parboil the green beans first.

SERVES 4
PREP TIME: 5 minutes
COOK TIME: 8 minutes

¼ cup water

2 teaspoons salt, divided

½ pound fresh greens beans, trimmed and halved

2 tablespoons canola oil

½ pound fresh white button mushrooms, quartered

2 teaspoons minced garlic

2 tablespoons hoisin sauce

1. In a wok, bring the water to a boil over high heat. Add 1 teaspoon of salt and the green beans. Cook, covered, for 3 minutes, or until the water evaporates.

2. With the wok still over high heat, add the oil, mushrooms, garlic, and the remaining 1 teaspoon of salt and stir-fry for 2 minutes.

3. Add the hoisin sauce, stir-fry for 2 more minutes, and serve.

SWAP IT: For a more authentic take, use chile broad bean paste instead of hoisin sauce and replace the salt with sugar. Broad bean paste is salty and spicy, which is why you don't need the salt.

Pan-Fried Black Pepper Tofu

**GLUTEN-FREE ❀ NUT-FREE ❀ VEGETARIAN ❀ 5 INGREDIENTS
FASTER THAN DELIVERY**

With plant-based diets becoming increasingly popular, people are turning to Asian cuisine for inspiration. Tofu is incredibly versatile and tastes great sautéed, deep-fried, pan-fried, grilled, or steamed. This tofu dish is a version of salt and pepper tofu. Instead of deep-frying, we pan-fry and bump up the black pepper for an extra kick of spice.

SERVES 4
PREP TIME: 5 minutes
COOK TIME: 10 minutes

1 (16-ounce) package medium-firm tofu, cut into 1-inch cubes

½ cup cornstarch

4 tablespoons canola oil

1 cup thinly sliced red onion

1 tablespoon minced garlic

1 teaspoon salt

2 tablespoons freshly ground black pepper

½ teaspoon sugar

1. Place the tofu in a large shallow dish. Add the cornstarch and toss to coat evenly.

2. In a cast-iron skillet, heat the oil over high heat. Add the tofu and pan-fry on all sides until golden brown, about 8 minutes. Transfer the tofu to paper towels to drain.

3. With the skillet still over high heat, add the onion and garlic and stir-fry for 1 minute.

4. Add the tofu, salt, pepper, and sugar and stir-fry for 1 more minute. Serve.

SERVING TIP: Enjoy this dish with rice or sautéed veggies, or serve it over a salad. Pair it with dipping sauces like sweet chile sauce or toasted sesame dressing and serve it as an appetizer.

Mixed Vegetable Stir-Fry

GLUTEN-FREE ❁ NUT-FREE ❁ VEGETARIAN ❁ FASTER THAN DELIVERY

In America, we like efficiency. We want to consume as many vegetables as possible in one sitting, be it in a salad, pressed juice, or smoothie. Because of this, mixed vegetable stir-fries became a very popular Chinese American dish.

SERVES 4
PREP TIME: 10 minutes
COOK TIME: 10 minutes

1 tablespoon canola oil

1 tablespoon thinly
 sliced ginger

2 garlic cloves, thinly sliced

1½ cups broccoli florets

2 cups quartered
 Roma tomatoes

¼ cup plus 1 teaspoon
 water, divided

1 cup snow peas

1½ cups sliced yellow
 bell peppers

1 teaspoon salt

½ teaspoon sugar

1 teaspoon cornstarch

2 teaspoons toasted
 sesame oil

1. In a wok, pour in the canola oil and heat on high. Add the ginger and garlic and stir-fry for 20 seconds.

2. Add the broccoli, tomatoes, and ¼ cup of water. Cover and cook for 5 minutes, or until the water has evaporated.

3. Add the peas, bell peppers, salt, and sugar and stir-fry for 3 minutes.

4. Mix together the cornstarch and remaining 1 teaspoon of water to make a slurry. Add it and the sesame oil to the wok and stir-fry for 1 minute. Serve.

TAKE A SHORTCUT: To cut down prep time, purchase precut vegetable stir-fry mix in a bag.

SWAP IT: Add a spicy kick to the stir-fry by swapping out the salt and sugar for 2 tablespoons of oyster sauce and 1 tablespoon of sriracha.

Sesame Bean Sprouts

GLUTEN-FREE ❁ **NUT-FREE** ❁ **SOY-FREE** ❁ **VEGETARIAN**
5 INGREDIENTS ❁ **FASTER THAN DELIVERY**

Korean cuisine is well-known for barbecue and *banchan,* the beautiful cold dishes that come with the meal. This dish is a popular banchan offering. It's aromatic, savory, and nutty without feeling heavy. It's a healthy side dish you can feel good about eating regularly.

SERVES 4 as a side
PREP TIME: 10 minutes
COOK TIME: 2 minutes

4 cups water

1 (12-ounce) bag
   bean sprouts

½ teaspoon salt

2 tablespoons toasted
   sesame oil

½ teaspoon minced garlic

¼ cup finely
   chopped scallions

1. In a stockpot, bring the water to a boil over high heat. Add the bean sprouts and cook for 2 minutes. Drain the bean sprouts in a colander and run under cold water for 1 minute to chill.

2. Squeeze the sprouts with your hands to remove excess water. Transfer them to a large mixing bowl.

3. Add the salt, oil, garlic, and scallions, tossing until well mixed. Serve.

SERVING TIP: The beauty of banchan is that it sits well in the refrigerator and can be eaten as leftovers. Toss leftover bean sprouts over rice to make Street Dog Bibimbap (page 52) or add them to a salad.

Vietnamese Pickled Carrots (Do Chua)

GLUTEN-FREE ✿ NUT-FREE ✿ SOY-FREE ✿ VEGETARIAN ✿ 5 INGREDIENTS

Pickled carrots are widely used in Vietnamese cuisine. They are often prepared with daikon and sometimes cucumbers. These sweet and sour crunchy vegetables appear on sandwiches, in rice noodle bowls, on imperial roll platters, and even on rice plates. To make this dish more accessible, the daikon has been omitted.

SERVES 4 as a side
PREP TIME: 10 minutes, plus 3 hours to pickle

2 (8-ounce) bags shredded carrots

2 teaspoons salt

2 cups sugar

1½ cups warm water

2 cups distilled white vinegar

1. In a large mixing bowl, put in the carrots. Add the salt, massage the carrots with your hands, then let them rest for 15 minutes.

2. Rinse the carrots under cold water, then drain the excess water.

3. In a medium mixing bowl, whisk the sugar in the water until the sugar dissolves. Whisk in the vinegar.

4. Fill clean glass mason jars three-quarters full with the carrots. Pour in the pickling liquid to cover.

5. Close the lids tightly and transfer to the refrigerator for at least 3 hours. Store in the refrigerator for up to 3 weeks.

SERVING TIPS: Toss some pickles on your hot dogs, place in your sandwiches, or even add some to your burger. Use them on your Street Dog Bibimbap (page 52), or pair them with other Vietnamese recipes found in this book.

Caramelized Brussels Sprouts

NUT-FREE ❁ SOY-FREE ❁ 5 INGREDIENTS ❁ FASTER THAN DELIVERY

Brussels sprouts have had a bad rap for years, but now you can find them on menus of all sorts, including those of Asian restaurants. In San Francisco and Los Angeles, fusion Vietnamese restaurants are adding stir-fried Brussels sprouts to their menus. The Asian twist on standard fried Brussels sprouts is the use of fish sauce and sugar, which packs a big punch of umami.

SERVES 4 as a side
PREP TIME: 5 minutes
COOK TIME: 12 minutes

6 cups plus 1 tablespoon water, divided

24 Brussels sprouts, quartered

¼ cup canola oil

4 garlic cloves, thinly sliced

2 teaspoons fish sauce

½ teaspoon salt

2 teaspoons sugar

1. In a stockpot, bring 6 cups of water to a boil over high heat. Add the sprouts and boil for 5 minutes. Drain the sprouts, wrap them with paper towels, and squeeze out excess water.

2. In a cast-iron skillet, pour in the oil and heat on high. Add half of the sprouts and stir-fry for 3 minutes. Transfer the sprouts to paper towels to drain. Repeat this process with the remaining half of sprouts.

3. Discard the oil from the skillet. Add the garlic and toast for 10 seconds.

4. Add the fish sauce, salt, sugar, the remaining 1 tablespoon of water, and all the sprouts. Toss the sprouts for 1 minute, until coated in sauce. Serve.

TAKE A SHORTCUT: To cut down on cooking time, use shredded Brussels sprouts. Simply omit the boiling step and go straight to stir-frying in oil.

Green Bean Omelet

NUT-FREE ❀ FASTER THAN DELIVERY

A Vietnamese omelet, or *trung chien*, is traditionally prepared with dried shrimp, fresh chiles, and minced scallions and served with rice or stuffed inside a baguette. It's called an omelet, but it's cooked more like a frittata. This Westernized version is milder than the traditional version, made with dried chile flakes instead of fresh chiles and fresh green beans instead of dried shrimp.

SERVES 4 as a side
PREP TIME: 5 minutes
COOK TIME: 5 minutes

2 teaspoons canola oil

1 cup minced green beans

6 eggs, whisked

1 tablespoon fish sauce

2 tablespoons soy sauce

1 teaspoon sugar

1 teaspoon dried
   chile flakes

1. In a nonstick sauté pan or skillet, pour in the oil and heat on high, swirling to coat.

2. Add the green beans and sauté for 2 minutes.

3. In a medium bowl, whisk together the eggs, fish sauce, soy sauce, sugar, and chile flakes.

4. Pour the egg mixture into the skillet, tilting if necessary, to allow the egg to coat the entire pan.

5. Reduce the heat to medium-low and poke holes in the cooked eggs to let the liquid run through. Cook for about 1 minute, or until the eggs set on top. Serve.

SERVING TIP: If the omelet technique is too hard to achieve, scrambling the eggs will work as well.

Eggplant with Green Curry

GLUTEN-FREE ❀ NUT-FREE ❀ SOY-FREE ❀ FASTER THAN DELIVERY

There are three types of curries in Thai cuisine: red, yellow, and green. Green curry is the most aromatic and herbaceous, as it has makrut lime, cilantro, and basil. These herbs give this mild curry its beautiful green color and its intoxicating aroma.

SERVES 4
PREP TIME: 10 minutes
COOK TIME: 10 minutes

¼ cup canola oil

2 Chinese eggplants, sliced 1-inch thick on the diagonal

2 tablespoons Thai green curry paste

1 (13.5-ounce) can full-fat coconut milk

1 tablespoon fish sauce

1 tablespoon sugar

½ cup water

1 (15-ounce) can baby corn, drained

1 cup snow peas

1. In a Dutch oven, pour in the oil and heat on high. Add the eggplant and stir-fry until the eggplant is soft when poked with a fork, about 5 minutes.

2. Transfer the eggplant to paper towels to drain. Discard the oil from the pot.

3. In the same Dutch oven still over high heat, whisk together the curry paste, coconut milk, fish sauce, sugar, and water and bring to a boil.

4. Add the baby corn, snow peas, and eggplant and cook for 3 minutes, until tender. Serve.

SWAP IT: To make this vegetarian, swap out the fish sauce for soy sauce.

SERVING TIP: Elevate the presentation of your dish to restaurant level by garnishing with lime wedges and fresh Thai bird's eye chiles.

Green Papaya Salad (Som Tum)

GLUTEN-FREE ✿ SOY-FREE ✿ FASTER THAN DELIVERY

This bright salad is traditionally mixed with fish sauce, limes, and dried shrimp or salted crab. Due to the pungent flavor of dried shrimp and crab, many Thai restaurants Westernize their green papaya salads by excluding them. This version follows suit and focuses on fresh herbs mixed with citrus, which makes it light, refreshing, and fragrant.

SERVES 4 as a side
PREP TIME: 15 minutes

1 green papaya

1 garlic clove, minced

1 tablespoon dried chile flakes

1 tablespoon fish sauce

1 tablespoon sugar

Juice of 1 lime

½ cup sliced cherry tomatoes

½ cup shredded carrots

2 tablespoons roasted peanuts

8 Thai basil leaves, julienned

1. Shred the papaya using the large holes of a box grater or julienne it with a chef's knife. Place the shredded papaya in a large mixing bowl.

2. To make the dressing, in a separate bowl, whisk together the garlic, chile flakes, fish sauce, sugar, and lime juice.

3. Pour the dressing over the papaya. Add the tomatoes, carrots, peanuts, and Thai basil, tossing until well-mixed. Serve.

SWAP IT: Swap green papaya for green apples. It tastes just as delicious and adds the same beautiful contrast to the salad you would get from a green papaya.

Okra and Eggs

GLUTEN-FREE ✿ NUT-FREE ✿ SOY-FREE ✿ FASTER THAN DELIVERY

This is a great introduction to Myanmarese cooking at home, as it's got all the flavors of authentic Myanmarese food but features very American ingredients. It's comfort food that's easy to make, due to a few shortcuts like frozen cut okra, canned tomatoes, and store-bought crispy onions.

SERVES 4
PREP TIME: 10 minutes
COOK TIME: 20 minutes

8 eggs

1 tablespoon canola oil

3 garlic cloves, thinly sliced

1 tablespoon dried
  chile flakes

½ teaspoon turmeric

½ teaspoon paprika

1 (24-ounce) can
  diced tomatoes

1 cup store-bought
  crispy onions

1 cup frozen okra

1 tablespoon fish sauce

½ teaspoon sugar

1 teaspoon salt

1. In a stockpot, put in the eggs and add water until the eggs are completely submerged. Bring to a boil over high heat and cook for 6 minutes. Pour out the water and run cold water over the eggs to chill them. Peel the eggs and set aside.

2. In a Dutch oven, pour in the oil and heat on high. Add the garlic, chile flakes, turmeric, and paprika and stir-fry for 10 seconds.

3. Add the tomatoes and bring to a boil. Reduce the heat to medium, add the peeled eggs, and simmer for 15 minutes.

4. Add the crispy onions, okra, fish sauce, sugar, and salt. Stir and simmer for 5 more minutes, until the okra is warmed through. Serve.

INGREDIENT TIP: I recommend French's crispy onions, but if you can't find them, any brand works.

Crispy Tofu with Peanut Sauce

VEGETARIAN ✿ FASTER THAN DELIVERY

Many sauces, dips, and dressings in Indonesian cuisine use peanuts. This sweet, savory, and creamy sauce paired with crispy tofu makes for an explosion of flavors and textures in one bite. And what's even better is this peanut sauce can be used over rice, noodles, dumplings, and salads.

SERVES 4
PREP TIME: 10 minutes
COOK TIME: 15 minutes

2 (16-ounce) packages medium-firm tofu, cut into 1-inch cubes

1 teaspoon salt

⅔ cup cornstarch

1 cup canola oil

½ cup peanut butter

¼ cup hot water

¼ cup soy sauce

¼ cup honey or maple syrup

1 tablespoon white vinegar

1. Place the tofu in a large bowl. Add the salt and cornstarch and toss to coat evenly.

2. In a cast-iron skillet, pour in the oil and heat on high. Working in batches to avoid overcrowding the pan, add the tofu and stir-fry for 4 minutes, or until golden brown. Transfer the tofu to paper towels to drain and set aside.

3. Whisk together the peanut butter and hot water in a bowl until smooth. Add the soy sauce, honey, and vinegar and whisk to combine.

4. Plate the tofu in a shallow bowl. Drizzle the peanut sauce on top and serve.

INGREDIENT TIP: Be sure to buy medium-firm tofu, as it produces the best results when fried. Firm tofu is too hard and silken tofu is too soft to handle.

Red Lentil Curry (Parippu)

**GLUTEN-FREE ❁ NUT-FREE ❁ SOY-FREE ❁ VEGETARIAN ❁ 5 INGREDIENTS
FASTER THAN DELIVERY ❁ ONE POT ❁ TAKEOUT FAVORITE**

Parippu is a traditional Sri Lankan dish that can be prepared with various types of lentils. It's traditionally cooked with coconut milk, turmeric, mustard seeds, fenugreek, cumin, and saffron and is commonly served alongside other dishes. For this recipe we use red lentils, as they cook faster than other lentils. To save money, this recipe calls for curry powder mix instead of five different spices.

SERVES 4
PREP TIME: 20 minutes
COOK TIME: 25 minutes

2 tablespoons canola oil

2 garlic cloves, minced

2 tablespoons Madras curry powder

8 ounces red lentils, rinsed and drained

1½ cups water

½ cup store-bought crispy onions

1 cup full-fat coconut milk

½ teaspoon salt

1 lime, quartered

1. In a Dutch oven, pour in the oil and heat on high. Add the garlic, curry powder, and lentils and stir-fry for 10 seconds. Add the water, bring to a boil, and cook for 20 minutes, until the lentils are tender.

2. Add the onions, coconut milk, and salt and cook, stirring, for 2 minutes.

3. Transfer the curry to a large serving bowl. Serve with lime for squeezing.

SWAP IT: Madras curry powder can be found at local supermarkets in the spice section. However, if it can't be found, garam masala, an Indian spice mix, works as well.

CHICKEN ADOBO, PAGE 108

SIX
Poultry

❁

Salt and Pepper Wings 101

Sweet and Sour Chicken 102

Kung Pao Chicken 103

Chicken with Green Beans in Garlic Sauce 104

Teriyaki Chicken 105

Chicken Karaage 106

Hainan Chicken and Rice 107

Chicken Adobo 108

Thai Basil Chicken (Pad Kra Pao Gai) 109

Mint Chicken 110

In Asia, poultry can be prepared in many different ways: poached, steamed, deep-fried, stir-fried, braised, roasted, smoked, grilled, and baked. As we can't focus on every technique, there are a few basic ones that can carry you through most Asian-inspired recipes. By learning to deep-fry, stir-fry, braise, and steam chicken, we can re-create most of the Asian American classics, from kung pao chicken to chicken teriyaki to chicken adobo. Given that poultry is the most consumed protein in America, adding 10 uniquely satisfying chicken recipes—with spicy, sweet, sour, herbaceous, and savory flavors inspired by Asia—to your repertoire of Sunday supper meals will make your family excited for more.

FUN ASIAN FOOD FACT

Poaching a whole chicken and serving it in its entirety is a distinctively Asian method of cooking poultry. In Chinese culture, the entire chicken from head to feet is served at the table, and this is because a whole chicken represents unity and must always be served during celebratory meals. Outside of large banquets, poached chicken is served as chicken and rice. Each Asian cuisine has its own version of this comfort food. Broth left over from poaching the chicken gets used to make Chicken Fat Rice (page 48), and the chicken is served over rice to make an inexpensive one-person meal, accompanied by a dipping sauce that changes depending on what area of Asia you are in. In Cantonese cuisine, minced ginger, garlic, and scallion in oil are used, while in Singapore, a dark soy sauce and chile-garlic sauce are used, as in Hainan Chicken and Rice (page 107).

Salt and Pepper Wings

**GLUTEN-FREE ❀ NUT-FREE ❀ SOY-FREE ❀ 5 INGREDIENTS
FASTER THAN DELIVERY**

Fried chicken is beloved across the world. In China, it's salt and pepper wings, which are seasoned with salt, pepper, fresh garlic, scallions, or chiles. They are crispy, juicy, and flavorful—and highly addictive.

SERVES 4
PREP TIME: 10 minutes, plus 30 minutes to marinate
COOK TIME: 25 minutes

16 chicken wings, midsection only

1 tablespoon sake or white wine

1½ teaspoons salt, divided

1½ teaspoons sugar, divided

8 tablespoons cornstarch, divided

5 cups canola oil

1 teaspoon freshly ground black pepper

1 jalapeño pepper, seeded and sliced

1. In a medium bowl, combine the chicken, sake, ½ teaspoon of salt, ½ teaspoon of sugar, and 2 tablespoons of cornstarch, tossing to coat well. Marinate for 30 minutes.

2. In a large cast-iron skillet, heat the oil over high heat to 350°F. Use a deep-fry thermometer to check the temperature.

3. While the oil heats, place the remaining 6 tablespoons of cornstarch in a shallow bowl. Dredge the wings in the cornstarch to evenly coat, then set aside.

4. Working in batches of 5 or 6 to avoid overcrowding the skillet, add the chicken and fry on each side for 4 minutes, or until golden brown. Transfer to paper towels to drain.

5. In a small bowl, whisk together the remaining 1 teaspoon of salt, remaining 1 teaspoon of sugar, and the pepper.

6. Season the wings with the pepper mix, garnish with the jalapeño, and serve.

> **INGREDIENT TIP:** Using only the midsection of the wings will cut down the cooking time.

Sweet and Sour Chicken

NUT-FREE ❁ FASTER THAN DELIVERY ❁ TAKEOUT FAVORITE

This iconic Chinese American dish is popular all over the world. People love the sauce so much it's used with many other dishes—even McDonald's offers it for chicken nuggets.

SERVES 4
PREP TIME: 10 minutes
COOK TIME: 10 minutes

2 chicken breasts, cut into 1-inch cubes

½ teaspoon salt

½ cup plus 1 tablespoon cornstarch, divided

5 cups canola oil

¼ cup ketchup

½ cup white vinegar

½ cup white sugar

¼ cup plus 1 tablespoon water, divided

1 tablespoon soy sauce

½ cup diced pineapple

1. In a medium bowl, combine the chicken, salt, and ½ cup of cornstarch, tossing to coat well. Set aside.

2. In a large cast-iron skillet, pour in the oil and heat on high to 350°F. Use a deep-fry thermometer to check the temperature.

3. Working in two batches to prevent overcrowding, add the chicken and fry on each side for 4 minutes, or until golden brown. Transfer to paper towels to drain.

4. In a saucepan over high heat, whisk together the ketchup, vinegar, sugar, ¼ cup of water, the soy sauce, and pineapple and bring to a boil.

5. Mix together the remaining 1 tablespoon of cornstarch and 1 tablespoon of water to make a slurry. Add it to the pan and stir until a thick, glossy sheen forms, 45 seconds to 1 minute.

6. Place the fried chicken in a serving bowl, pour in the sauce, and toss to coat evenly. Serve.

SWAP IT: Swap chicken for pork tenderloin to make sweet and sour pork.

Kung Pao Chicken

NUT-FREE ✿ FASTER THAN DELIVERY ✿ TAKEOUT FAVORITE

This classic Sichuan stir-fry is traditionally made with numbing Sichuan peppercorns, bone-in chicken, and tons of chiles. The American version omits the peppercorns, brings down the spice level, and uses boneless white meat chicken.

SERVES 4
PREP TIME: 10 minutes
COOK TIME: 10 minutes

2 chicken breasts, diced

1 tablespoon soy sauce

¼ cup plus 1 teaspoon cornstarch, divided

1 tablespoon canola oil

3 slices ginger

¼ cup roasted peanuts

1 tablespoon dark soy sauce

1½ teaspoons salt

1 tablespoon black vinegar

1 teaspoon sugar

1 teaspoon dried chile flakes

1 teaspoon water

¼ cup scallions

1. In a medium bowl, combine the chicken, soy sauce, and ¼ cup of cornstarch, tossing to coat well. Set aside.

2. In a wok, pour in the oil and heat on high. Add the chicken and ginger and stir-fry for 5 minutes.

3. Add the peanuts, soy sauce, salt, vinegar, sugar, and chile flakes and stir-fry for 3 minutes.

4. Mix together the remaining 1 teaspoon of cornstarch and the water to make a slurry. Add it and the scallions to the wok and stir for 2 minutes, or until sauce thickens and absorbs into the chicken. Serve.

SWAP IT: Swap chicken for shrimp to make kung pao shrimp.

Chicken with Green Beans in Garlic Sauce

GLUTEN-FREE ❁ NUT-FREE ❁ SOY-FREE ❁ FASTER THAN DELIVERY

Chicken with String Beans is a very Chinese American Dish. String beans or green beans are a very American vegetable and, when paired with white meat chicken, makes it very approachable. Garlic sauce is a white sauce, meaning that it does not contain soy sauce. It's gluten-free and much lighter than your typical stir-fry.

SERVES 4
PREP TIME: 5 minutes
COOK TIME: 12 minutes

2 chicken breasts, cut into 1-inch cubes

1 tablespoon plus 1 teaspoon cornstarch, divided

1½ teaspoons salt, divided

1½ teaspoons sugar, divided

1 tablespoon canola oil

1½ cups green beans, trimmed and cut into 2-inch pieces

3 garlic cloves, minced

2 tablespoons plus 1 teaspoon water, divided

1. In a medium bowl, combine the chicken, 1 tablespoon of cornstarch, ½ teaspoon of salt, and ½ teaspoon of sugar, tossing to coat well. Set aside.

2. In a wok, pour in the oil and heat on high. Add the chicken and stir-fry for 6 minutes. Remove the chicken from the wok and set aside.

3. Add the green beans, garlic, the remaining 1 teaspoon of salt, the remaining 1 teaspoon of sugar, and 2 tablespoons of water. Stir, cover, and cook for 4 minutes. Add the chicken back into the wok.

4. Mix together the remaining 1 teaspoon of cornstarch and 1 teaspoon of water to make a slurry. Add it to the wok and stir-fry for 2 minutes, until the sauce thickens. Serve.

SWAP IT: Swap the salt with 2 tablespoons of black bean sauce to make chicken in black bean sauce. Swap green beans for asparagus or sugar snap peas.

Teriyaki Chicken

NUT-FREE 🏵 FASTER THAN DELIVERY 🏵 TAKEOUT FAVORITE

Teriyaki is one of the most well-known sauces in Japanese cuisine. This sweet, salty, caramel-like sauce is usually prepared with beef or chicken and served over rice. Pair this delicious dish with a side of vegetables, and you've got yourself the perfect meal.

SERVES 4
PREP TIME: 5 minutes
COOK TIME: 10 minutes

4 chicken breast cutlets, pounded thin

¼ cup plus 2 tablespoons soy sauce, divided

2 tablespoons mirin, sake, or dry white wine

2 tablespoons toasted sesame oil

1 tablespoon canola oil

7 tablespoons brown sugar

½ teaspoon minced ginger

1 cup plus 2 teaspoons water, divided

2 teaspoons cornstarch

1. In a medium bowl, marinate the chicken in 2 tablespoons of soy sauce, the mirin, and sesame oil.

2. In a wok, pour in the canola oil and heat on high. Add 2 cutlets and pan-fry on each side for 2 minutes. Transfer to paper towels to drain. Repeat this process with the remaining 2 cutlets.

3. In the wok, still over high heat, combine the sugar, the remaining ¼ cup of soy sauce, ginger, and 1 cup of water and boil for 5 minutes.

4. Mix together the cornstarch and remaining 2 teaspoons of water to make a slurry. Add it to the wok and stir for 2 minutes, until the sauce thickens.

5. Add the chicken and cook on each side for 2 minutes. Serve.

SERVING TIP: If you have a grill, grill the chicken cutlets. The smokiness of the chicken paired with teriyaki sauce creates a burnt caramel sweetness.

Chicken Karaage

NUT-FREE

Karaage is a deep-fried dish that coats protein or vegetables in potato starch and fries them until crispy. Chicken is the most common type of karaage in the United States, but in Japan, it's often made with seafood.

SERVES 4
PREP TIME: 10 minutes, plus 1 hour to marinate
COOK TIME: 10 minutes

4 skin-on boneless chicken thighs, cut into bite-size pieces

⅓ cup soy sauce

2 tablespoons sake

Juice of 1 lemon

2 garlic cloves, minced

5 cups canola oil

1½ cups potato flour

1 teaspoon sea salt

1. Place the chicken in a medium bowl. Add the soy sauce, sake, lemon juice, and garlic and use your hands to mix in the marinade. Let it marinate for 1 hour.

2. In a large cast-iron skillet, pour in the oil and heat to 340°F. Use a deep-fry thermometer to check the temperature.

3. Place the flour in a shallow bowl. Dredge the chicken in the flour.

4. Working in batches to avoid overcrowding the skillet, add the chicken and fry until golden brown, about 7 minutes. Transfer the chicken to a wire rack to drain.

5. Season the chicken with salt while still hot and serve.

SWAP IT: Potato flour produces the lightest, fluffiest coating and is traditionally used in chicken karaage, but if you can't find it, all-purpose flour or cornstarch work well.

Hainan Chicken and Rice

GLUTEN-FREE ✤ NUT-FREE

Chicken and rice has blown up in America in the last few years. But the true godfather of it all is Savoy in Los Angeles. This spot opened in 1982 and serves its famous Hainan Chicken and Rice, alongside pizza with conch and prosciutto, curry beef stews, and roasted chicken over pasta.

SERVES 4
PREP TIME: 20 minutes
COOK TIME: 45 minutes

6 cups plus 4 tablespoons water, divided

4 skin-on boneless chicken thighs

4 skin-on chicken breasts

6 slices ginger

1 scallion, halved

2 tablespoons salt

3 pandan leaves or bay leaves

Juice of 2 limes

4 teaspoons sugar

6 tablespoons sriracha

6 garlic cloves

2 tablespoons minced ginger

Chicken Fat Rice (page 48), for serving

1. In a stockpot over high heat, pour in 6 cups of water. Add the chicken, ginger slices, scallion, salt, and pandan leaves and bring to a boil. Reduce the heat to medium, cover, and simmer for 40 minutes, or until the chicken is cooked through.

2. Combine the remaining 4 tablespoons of water, the lime juice, sugar, sriracha, garlic, and minced ginger in a blender and pulse until smooth.

3. Remove the chicken from the pot and plunge it into an ice bath for 30 seconds.

4. Slice the chicken into ½-inch strips. Serve over Chicken Fat Rice with the sauce.

> **SWAP IT:** Use skinless chicken if you prefer, as poached chicken skin isn't for everyone.

Chicken Adobo

NUT-FREE ❀ FASTER THAN DELIVERY ❀ ONE POT ❀ TAKEOUT FAVORITE

Chicken adobo is one of the most popular Filipino dishes. It's prepared with bay leaves, black peppercorns, soy sauce, sugar, and vinegar. The sauce in adobo works beautifully with rice or mashed potatoes.

SERVES 4
PREP TIME: 5 minutes
COOK TIME: 40 minutes

2 tablespoons canola oil

4 skin-on, bone-in chicken thighs

¼ cup soy sauce

½ cup white vinegar

1 tablespoon sugar

1 teaspoon whole black peppercorns

2 bay leaves

3 garlic cloves, sliced

1. In a Dutch oven, pour in the oil and heat on high. Add the chicken and fry on each side for 3 minutes, until golden brown.

2. Add the soy sauce, vinegar, sugar, peppercorns, bay leaves, and garlic and bring to a boil. Reduce the heat to low, cover, and simmer for 20 minutes.

3. Turn the chicken over, cover, and cook for another 10 minutes, or until the chicken is cooked through.

4. Uncover, increase the heat to high, and cook until the sauce thickens, about 5 minutes. Serve.

SERVING TIP: Shred leftover adobo chicken and use it to make tacos or burritos for a fun Filipino Mexican dish.

Thai Basil Chicken (Pad Kra Pao Gai)

NUT-FREE ❀ FASTER THAN DELIVERY ❀ ONE POT

This is a popular Thai street-food dish served with rice and fried egg. *Pad kra pao* means "stir-fried holy basil" and *gai* means "chicken." Holy basil is not to be confused with Thai basil, which is more pungent in flavor than holy basil. This version uses Italian basil because it resembles holy basil more than Thai basil.

SERVES 4
PREP TIME: 3 minutes
COOK TIME: 20 minutes

1 tablespoon canola oil

1 pound ground chicken

5 Thai chiles

3 garlic cloves, minced

1 tablespoon oyster sauce

1 tablespoon soy sauce

1 tablespoon fish sauce

1 teaspoon dark soy sauce

1 teaspoon sugar

1 cup chopped fresh basil

1. In a wok, pour in the oil and heat on high. Add the chicken and stir-fry for 5 minutes, breaking the chicken apart with a spatula.

2. Add the chiles, garlic, oyster sauce, soy sauce, fish sauce, dark soy sauce, and sugar and stir-fry for 3 minutes.

3. Add the basil and stir fry for 2 minutes. Serve.

SWAP IT: If Thai chiles can't be found, use 2 teaspoons sambal, an Indonesian chile paste, or sriracha instead.

Mint Chicken

NUT-FREE ❁ FASTER THAN DELIVERY ❁ TAKEOUT FAVORITE

Myanmarese-style mint chicken is sort of like taco-style ground beef, except made with Southeast Asian flavors. The fresh mint added in the end reminds me of fresh cilantro and onions tossed on top of tacos. This flavorful chicken dish can be enjoyed with rice and in tortillas and lettuce cups.

SERVES 4
PREP TIME: 15 minutes
COOK TIME: 10 minutes

1 tablespoon canola oil

1 pound ground chicken

½ teaspoon cumin powder

1 tablespoon sambal

1 tablespoon dark soy sauce

1 teaspoon fish sauce

½ teaspoon sugar

1 tablespoon minced garlic

½ cup chopped fresh mint

1. In a wok, pour in the oil and heat on high. Add the chicken and cumin and stir-fry for 5 minutes, breaking the chicken apart with a spatula.

2. Add the sambal, soy sauce, fish sauce, sugar, and garlic and stir-fry for 5 minutes.

3. Garnish with the mint and serve.

INGREDIENT TIP: Sambal is an Indonesian chile paste made with shrimp paste, garlic, ginger, shallots, sugar, and lime juice. Find it in the Asian section of the grocery or online.

SWAP IT: Swap sambal for red curry paste, which has similar flavors. Add extra sugar and a touch of fish sauce to balance out the flavors.

SWEET AND SPICY KOREAN SHORT RIBS (GALBI), PAGE 125

SEVEN
Beef, Pork, and Lamb

Chicken may be the most popular protein in the United States, but pork is the most consumed meat in China. From dumpling fillings and stir-fried dishes to soups and braises, pork is used more than any other protein. It is prized for its sweet, mild flavor and pleasant texture. And that's why half the recipes in this chapter are dedicated to pork prepared in every which way: ground pork, pork chops, pork shoulder, bacon, and sausages. While bacon and sausages are not conventional ingredients in Asian cuisine, they pair beautifully with Asian flavors and provide great shortcuts to save time. Mixing Western and Asian ingredients is what this book is all about. Dishes such as kung pao pastrami from the famous Mission Chinese Food in San Francisco prove that Western substitutes, such as pastrami, bacon, and Italian sausage, can be used to create delicious mainstream Asian American dishes. You'll also learn to use certain Asian seasonings like a pro. Hoisin sauce, soy sauce, and chile bean sauce are a few versatile sauces you'll start stocking in your pantry.

FUN ASIAN FOOD FACT

According to Chinese medicine, seasonal eating promotes good health. There is a whole school of thought that explains which ingredients should be consumed during the winter versus during the summer. When it's cold, your body needs heat and increased blood flow to bring energy and strength. During the hot seasons, your body needs to cool down, cleanse, and rehydrate to feel less heavy, lethargic, and weak. Proteins such as lamb, beef, and pork are consumed largely in Northern China, where there are freezing winters. Meat dishes combined with spices such as cumin, garlic, and peppercorn all bring heat to your body and get your blood flowing. Sichuan Lamb with Scallions (page 116) and Mapo Tofu with Pork (page 120) are examples of dishes from the Sichuan region that will keep you warm and satisfied. Korea also has cold winters, which explains why grilling meats over charcoal is so popular, as are stews and soups. Sitting by a grill, cooking your own Sweet and Spicy Korean Short Ribs (page 125) with a hot bowl of rice is the perfect way to prepare a winter meal. In contrast, if you head to Vietnam and Singapore, where the weather is hot, dishes such as Grass Jelly Almond Ice-Cream Float (page 151) or Honeydew Sago (page 152) will help cleanse the system of heat and provide hydration.

Sichuan Lamb with Scallions

NUT-FREE ✿ FASTER THAN DELIVERY

In Northern China, regions such as Sichuan, Hebei, Shanxi, and Beijing favor garlic, scallions, and chiles. The region's food tends to be simple, mostly meat-based, and limited in the harsh winter months when it comes to veggies. Americans' tolerance for spice has gone up over the years, and spicier regional dishes such as this one are becoming staples.

SERVES 4
PREP TIME: 12 minutes
COOK TIME: 8 minutes

1 pound boneless lamb, thinly sliced

2 teaspoons cornstarch

½ teaspoon salt

2 garlic cloves, sliced

1 teaspoon ground cumin

2 tablespoons soy sauce

1 tablespoon Shaoxing rice wine or dry white wine

1½ teaspoons canola oil

2 teaspoons Sichuan peppercorns

1½ cups sliced scallions

2 tablespoons dried chile flakes

1. In a large bowl, marinate the lamb with the cornstarch, salt, garlic, cumin, soy sauce, and wine for 10 minutes.

2. In a wok, pour in the oil and heat on medium. Add the peppercorns and sauté for 2 minutes to release their flavor. Remove and discard the peppercorns but leave the oil.

3. Increase the heat to high to heat the oil. Add the lamb, scallions, and chile flakes. Stir-fry for 5 minutes, until the lamb is cooked through, and serve.

INGREDIENT TIP: Shaoxing rice wine is a type of Chinese rice wine. Find it in the Asian section of some supermarkets and in Asian markets.

SWAP IT: Sichuan peppercorns provide the characteristic numbing effect of Sichuan cuisine, but they can be hard to find. If necessary, swap them with whole black peppercorns.

Mongolian Beef

NUT-FREE ❁ FASTER THAN DELIVERY ❁ TAKEOUT FAVORITE

Mongolian beef is not actually from Mongolia. It was made popular in the United States by Chinese restaurants, where sautéing in a round griddle in front of customers became a huge fast-casual hit during the 1980s.

SERVES 4
PREP TIME: 10 minutes
COOK TIME: 10 minutes

1 pound flank steak, thinly sliced

3 tablespoons cornstarch, divided

3 tablespoons toasted sesame oil

1 teaspoon salt

2 teaspoons canola oil

1½ cups baby corn

2 tablespoons soy sauce

6 tablespoons hoisin sauce

2 tablespoons white vinegar

1 tablespoon sugar

2 tablespoons freshly ground black pepper

1 tablespoon water

1. Marinate the steak with 2 tablespoons of cornstarch, the sesame oil, and salt for 2 minutes.

2. In a wok, pour in the canola oil and heat on high. Add the beef and stir-fry for 5 minutes. Transfer to a plate.

3. In the same wok still over high heat, add the baby corn, soy sauce, hoisin sauce, vinegar, sugar, and pepper and stir-fry for 4 minutes.

4. Mix together the remaining 1 tablespoon of cornstarch and the water to make a slurry. Add it and the beef to the wok and stir-fry until the sauce thickens, about 1 minute.

SWAP IT: Swap baby corn with any crunchy vegetable you like that cooks fast, such as snow peas, celery, or bell peppers.

Beef and Broccoli

NUT-FREE ❁ FASTER THAN DELIVERY ❁ TAKEOUT FAVORITE

Beef and broccoli is a quintessential Chinese American dish that was created after the original version called *gai lan chao niu rou*. The Cantonese version uses Chinese broccoli, something that wasn't available in the United States back in the early days.

SERVES 4
PREP TIME: 15 minutes
COOK TIME: 16 minutes

6 ounces broccoli florets

4 tablespoons canola oil, divided

1 pound boneless ribeye steak, cut into 1-inch cubes

2 tablespoons cornstarch

2 tablespoons white wine

1 teaspoon salt

1 teaspoon sugar

½ cup oyster sauce

1 teaspoon ginger powder or fresh minced ginger

¼ cup soy sauce

¼ cup honey

3 tablespoons water

1. Preheat the oven to 350°F.

2. In a medium bowl, toss the broccoli in 2 tablespoons of oil and transfer it to a baking sheet.

3. Marinate the beef in the cornstarch, wine, salt, and sugar for 10 minutes.

4. While the beef is marinating, roast the broccoli for 10 minutes, then transfer to a serving plate and set aside.

5. In a wok, pour in the remaining 2 tablespoons of oil and heat on high. Add the beef and stir-fry until medium done, about 5 minutes. Plate the beef over the broccoli.

6. In the same wok still over high heat, combine the oyster sauce, ginger, soy sauce, honey, and water and simmer, stirring, for 1 minute.

7. Pour the sauce over the beef and broccoli and serve.

INGREDIENT TIP: Roasting broccoli creates a nutty, slightly charred flavor that works beautifully with beef and broccoli sauce. Boiling broccoli, which is the traditional method, can produce watery stir-fry results.

Spicy Twice-Cooked Bacon

NUT-FREE ❀ FASTER THAN DELIVERY ❀ ONE POT

Twice-cooked pork, called *hui guo rou,* is a traditional Sichuan dish. Pork belly is first boiled whole, then sliced thin before being sautéed in a hot wok. This version uses bacon, which eliminates the need to cook the pork twice and adds a smoky flavor to the dish.

SERVES 4
PREP TIME: 5 minutes
COOK TIME: 8 minutes

1 teaspoon canola oil

12 bacon slices, cut into 2-inch pieces

1 leek, thinly sliced at an angle

5 thin slices ginger

1 (8-ounce) can water chestnuts, drained

1 tablespoon white wine

1 tablespoon chile bean sauce, such as Lee Kum Kee

1 tablespoon brown sugar

1 teaspoon dried chile flakes

1. In a wok, pour in the oil and heat on high. Add the bacon and cook until slightly crisp, about 3 minutes. Transfer the bacon to paper towels to drain.

2. Add the leek, ginger, water chestnuts, and wine and sauté for 3 minutes.

3. Add the bean sauce, sugar, chile flakes, and bacon and stir-fry for 2 minutes. Serve.

INGREDIENT TIP: The addition of water chestnuts sweetens up the dish a bit and adds a layer of moist crunch to the dish to complement the salty, oily bacon.

Mapo Tofu with Pork

**NUT-FREE ❀ 5 INGREDIENTS ❀ FASTER THAN DELIVERY
ONE POT ❀ TAKEOUT FAVORITE**

The word *ma* is short for *ma-zi,* which means "pockmarks," and the Chinese word *popo* means "grandma." Many believe a pockmarked old woman came up with this dish, thus "mapo" tofu was born. The Sichuan version uses salty broad bean paste and numbing peppercorns. This one uses Italian sausage, which imparts a surprisingly authentic taste.

SERVES 4
PREP TIME: 10 minutes
COOK TIME: 8 minutes

2 teaspoons canola oil

4 spicy Italian sausages, casings removed

1 (16-ounce) package medium-firm tofu, cut into 1-inch cubes

2 tablespoons soy sauce

1 tablespoon chile powder

1 tablespoon toasted sesame oil

1. In a wok, pour in the canola oil and heat on high. Add the sausage and stir-fry for 3 minutes, breaking the sausage apart with a spatula.

2. Add the tofu, soy sauce, and chile powder and gently stir to combine.

3. Reduce the heat to medium and simmer for 5 minutes.

4. Add the sesame oil, stir to combine, and serve.

INGREDIENT TIP: To add the authentic numbing element, start the recipe by toasting Sichuan peppercorns in the oil. Remove the peppercorns, then use the oil to cook the sausage.

Lemongrass Pork Chops (Thit Heo Nuong Xa)

NUT-FREE

You can smell this dish in the streets of Vietnam from miles away. This cheap, everyday dish is now a healthy fast-casual concept for Americans, where you can choose from grilled lemongrass chicken, pork, or beef served over a bowl of rice, noodles, or salad. This recipe calls for a skillet, but if you have a grill, throw those chops on there.

SERVES 4
PREP TIME: 5 minutes, plus 4 hours to marinate
COOK TIME: 8 minutes

½ cup fish sauce

2 tablespoons soy sauce

¼ cup honey

2 garlic cloves, minced

Juice of 1 lime

2 tablespoons lemongrass paste

4 bone-in pork chops

2 tablespoons canola oil

1. In a large bowl, whisk together the fish sauce, soy sauce, honey, garlic, lime juice, and lemongrass. Add the pork chops and cover with the marinade. Transfer to the refrigerator to marinate overnight or for at least 4 hours.

2. Let the pork rest at room temperature for 30 minutes. Remove the pork chops from the marinade and pat dry. Reserve the marinade.

3. In a large cast-iron skillet, pour in the oil and heat on high. Add the pork chops and sear on each side for 4 minutes. Add the marinade and cook the pork chops for 2 minutes on each side, or until they are cooked through.

4. Transfer the pork chops to plates, pour the sauce on top, and serve.

TAKE A SHORTCUT: To cut down on cooking time and to save 2 hours of marinating time, choose thin chops over thick cuts.

Shaking Beef (Bo Luc Lac)

NUT-FREE ❀ TAKEOUT FAVORITE

This dish gets its name from the shaking motion used to cook the beef in a wok. In the United States, this dish appears more often at higher-end Vietnamese restaurants touting chunkier expensive cuts such as filet mignon or ribeye. In Vietnam, large chunks of sautéed beef are not desired and high-quality meats are not affordable, so they use cheaper cuts that are tougher and thus cut small.

SERVES 4
PREP TIME: 5 minutes, plus 2 hours to marinate
COOK TIME: 8 minutes

1 teaspoon sugar

2 tablespoons fish sauce

1 teaspoon dark soy sauce

1 tablespoon soy sauce

1 tablespoon freshly ground black pepper

Juice of 1 lime

1 pound filet mignon, cut into ¾-inch cubes

2 tablespoons canola oil

1 small red onion, thinly sliced, for garnish

1 lime, cut into wedges

1. In a large bowl, whisk together the sugar, fish sauce, dark soy sauce, soy sauce, pepper, and lime juice. Add the steak, mix to coat, and marinate in the refrigerator for 2 hours.

2. In a large cast-iron skillet, pour in the oil and heat on high. Add the steak and sear on each side for 1 minute by shaking the pan every minute for a total of 4 minutes.

3. Plate the steak, garnish with the onion and limes, and serve.

> **SERVING TIP:** If medium-rare is not desired, cook the steak for 4 minutes longer for medium-well.

Spicy Pork Patties

GLUTEN-FREE ❀ NUT-FREE ❀ SOY-FREE ❀ FASTER THAN DELIVERY

The flavors of this patty capture the brightness of Northern Thai sausages. Traditionally, Thai sausages are eaten with sticky rice or as an appetizer. To make these sausages more approachable, we turned them into little patties. Now you can enjoy them as mini sliders, in lettuce wraps, or over rice.

SERVES 4
PREP TIME: 30 minutes
COOK TIME: 8 minutes

¾ pound ground pork

2 teaspoons Thai red curry paste

2 teaspoons cornstarch

1 small red onion, finely chopped

2 tablespoons lime juice

¼ cup minced fresh cilantro

2 teaspoons sugar

1 tablespoon dried chile flakes

2 teaspoons fish sauce

½ cup canola oil

1. In a large bowl, using your hands, mix together the pork, curry paste, cornstarch, onion, lime juice, cilantro, sugar, chile flakes, and fish sauce. Cover and chill for 30 minutes.

2. Form the pork mixture into patties by dividing it into 12 equal portions. Roll each portion into a ball, then flatten it into a ½-inch-thick disk.

3. In a large cast-iron skillet, pour in the oil and heat on high until the oil smokes. Reduce the heat to medium, add the patties, and shallow-fry on each side for 4 minutes, or until cooked through. Transfer to paper towels to drain. Serve

SWAP IT: If you don't like pork, you can swap it for ground chicken or turkey.

Pork Bulgogi

NUT-FREE ❁ FASTER THAN DELIVERY ❁ TAKEOUT FAVORITE

In Korea, spicy pork bulgogi (*dwaeji bulgogi*) is far more popular than beef bulgogi, though the beef version dominates in America. The traditional sauce is spicy from gochujang and sweet from sugar and pureed apple or Korean pear. This version uses canned pears, which are readily available everywhere and produce the same results. Enjoy over rice or in lettuce wraps.

SERVES 4
PREP TIME: 35 minutes
COOK TIME: 10 minutes

1 (8-ounce) can
    pears, drained

4 tablespoons gochujang

3 tablespoons soy sauce

3 tablespoons brown sugar

1 tablespoon minced ginger

2 tablespoons toasted
    sesame oil

1 teaspoon freshly ground
    black pepper

1 pound pork shoulder,
    thinly sliced

1 tablespoon canola oil

1 medium white onion,
    thinly sliced

2 tablespoons toasted
    sesame seeds

1. In a blender, combine the pears, gochujang, soy sauce, sugar, ginger, sesame oil, and pepper and pulse for 20 seconds, or until smooth. In a large bowl, combine the pork and the sauce and marinate for 30 minutes.

2. In a wok, pour in the canola oil and heat on high until the oil smokes. Reduce the heat to medium, add the pork, and stir-fry for 8 minutes. Add the onion and stir-fry for 2 minutes.

3. Garnish with the sesame seeds and serve.

> **SWAP IT:** At Korean markets you can find presliced pork shoulder, but you can also ask your butcher for this cut. But if your butcher can't supply this cut, then getting pork tenderloin and slicing it yourself will work as well.

Sweet and Spicy Korean Short Ribs (Galbi)

NUT-FREE

The word *galbi* means "ribs" in Korean. In Korea, short ribs are cut along the bone, resulting in a thick piece of meat with one bone. In America, we know Korean short ribs as thin strips of meat with three bones in it. This cut was created by Koreans here in Los Angeles.

SERVES 4
PREP TIME: 5 minutes, plus 4 hours to marinate
COOK TIME: 8 minutes

½ cup brown sugar

4 tablespoons toasted sesame oil

½ cup canned pineapple, drained

5 garlic cloves, minced

½ cup soy sauce

2 teaspoons vinegar

2 teaspoons Korean chile powder (gochugaru) or sriracha

4 pounds Korean short ribs (see Tip on page 62)

1. In a blender, combine the sugar, sesame oil, pineapple, garlic, soy sauce, vinegar, and chile powder and pulse for 15 seconds, or until smooth.

2. Place the ribs and marinade in a 2-gallon zip-top bag and marinate for 4 hours in the refrigerator.

3. Let the ribs rest for 30 minutes at room temperature. Remove them from the marinade and reserve the marinade.

4. Heat a gas or charcoal grill to medium. Add the ribs and grill on each side for 4 minutes, or until cooked through. Set aside on a serving plate.

5. Transfer the marinade to a saucepot over high heat and bring to a boil. Cook for 3 minutes. Serve the ribs with the sauce on the side.

INGREDIENT TIP: Traditionally, Asian pears are used in the marinade, but when you can't find them, canned pineapple does the trick.

TUNA POKE BOWL, PAGE 134

EIGHT
Seafood

Steamed Scallops with Ginger and Scallions 129

Salt and Pepper Calamari 130

Honey Walnut Shrimp 131

Wasabi Soy Salmon 132

Hibachi Garlic Prawns 133

Tuna Poke Bowl 134

Sugarcane Shrimp 135

Fish in Caramel Sauce (Ca Kho To) 136

Coconut Clams with Lime 137

Fried Tilapia with Salsa 138

Seafood is a major part of the Asian diet, especially in the southern regions of Asia where island and coastal cultures have made it a signature ingredient. As a result, all kinds of seafood can be found in Asia, varying from region to region. Different seafood means different sauces and methods of cooking, resulting in a foodie paradise for seafood lovers. For example, clams in Thailand may be sautéed or boiled with lemongrass, coconut, and galangal while clams in Hong Kong may be stir-fried with chile black beans. Fish may be poached in spicy broth in Northern China but braised in a caramel fish sauce in Vietnam. This chapter will show you how to make a wide variety of Asian-style seafood dishes with an American twist. You'll learn to steam, fry, braise, and stir-fry seafood to master your favorite Asian American dishes from the comfort of your home.

FUN ASIAN FOOD FACT

Did you know that fish is often served whole, from head to tail, in Asia? And that almost all seafood consumed is usually live or freshly caught and never frozen? Asians value freshness at such a high level that seafood restaurants are outfitted with tanks carrying live sea creatures for customers to choose from. You can order crab, lobster, fish, mollusks, shrimp, and eel, just to name a few, by weight from the tank, then choose a preparation method, and sit down for a feast. Delicate-fleshed fish are usually steamed with aromatics so the true flavor of the fish can come through. The fatty meat closest to the fin, tail, and head is the tastiest. A firmer-fleshed fish can be deep-fried, sautéed, or braised. If you feel adventurous, try making Fried Tilapia with Salsa (page 138) using a whole fish, which is the traditional way.

Steamed Scallops with Ginger and Scallions

NUT-FREE ✿ 5 INGREDIENTS ✿ FASTER THAN DELIVERY

Steamed fish, prawns, and scallops are common in Chinese cuisine, especially in the southern region of China, where sauces are light and used to bring out the natural flavors of the fish. When this method of cooking was brought to the United States, restaurant owners used prepped seafood that Americans recognized—sea bass, salmon, scallops, and peeled prawns—as they were concerned seafood with bones, heads, and tails would be too exotic.

SERVES 4
PREP TIME: 5 minutes
COOK TIME: 5 minutes

4 cups water

12 fresh scallops

1 (2-inch) piece ginger, thinly sliced

½ cup thinly sliced scallions

2 tablespoons soy sauce

2 tablespoons canola oil

1. In a stockpot fitted with a steaming rack, bring the water to a boil over high heat.

2. Slice each scallop in half and place on a shallow round plate, spreading them out evenly.

3. Using oven mitts, place the plate on the steaming rack. Cover and steam for 3 minutes.

4. Remove the plate, garnish with the ginger and scallions, and pour the soy sauce over the top.

5. In a small pan, pour in the oil and heat on high. Then pour the hot oil over the scallops and serve.

SWAP IT: Swap the scallops with tender whitefish fillets, such as dover sole or sea bass.

Salt and Pepper Calamari

**GLUTEN-FREE ❀ NUT-FREE ❀ SOY-FREE ❀ 5 INGREDIENTS
FASTER THAN DELIVERY**

In Chinese cuisine, there is a method of preparation called "salt and pepper," where ingredients are fried and seasoned in a salt and pepper mix, then tossed with aromatics such as garlic and fresh chiles. With America's love for fried calamari, it's no wonder that this dish has become a huge hit.

SERVES 4
PREP TIME: 5 minutes
COOK TIME: 6 minutes

1 pound fresh calamari

1 egg, whisked

¼ cup cornstarch

1½ cups canola oil

3 teaspoons salt

1 teaspoon freshly ground black pepper

1 teaspoon sugar

1 jalapeño pepper, seeded and minced

1. Place the calamari in a large bowl. Add the egg and use your hands to mix. Add the cornstarch and mix again to coat evenly.

2. In a Dutch oven, pour in the oil and heat on high to 375°F. Use a deep-fry thermometer to check the temperature.

3. Working in batches to avoid overcrowding the pot, add the calamari and fry for 2 to 3 minutes, or golden brown. Transfer the calamari to paper towels to drain, then plate.

4. In a small bowl, combine the salt, pepper, and sugar. Sprinkle the mix over the calamari, garnish with the jalapeño, and serve.

SERVING TIP: Don't use the entire salt and pepper mix on this dish. Sprinkle some on, taste, and add more as needed. Serve leftover mix on the side for guests who want more.

Honey Walnut Shrimp

GLUTEN-FREE ❁ **SOY-FREE** ❁ **FASTER THAN DELIVERY**

Honey walnut shrimp was invented in Hong Kong under the influence of British colonization. Crispy sweet prawns paired with candied walnuts was a match made in heaven, and when the chefs in Hong Kong brought it over to the United States, it quickly became a Chinese American staple.

SERVES 4
PREP TIME: 10 minutes
COOK TIME: 6 minutes

20 medium shrimp, peeled and deveined

1 teaspoon salt

2 eggs, whisked

1 cup cornstarch

1½ cups canola oil

½ cup mayonnaise

¼ honey

2 tablespoons heavy (whipping) cream

1 cup store-bought candied walnuts

1. In a medium bowl, combine the shrimp, salt, and eggs and use your hands to massage to coat evenly.

2. Pour the cornstarch into a shallow bowl. Dredge the shrimp in the cornstarch and set aside.

3. In a Dutch oven, pour in the oil and heat on high to 350°F. Use a deep-fry thermometer to check the temperature.

4. Working in batches to avoid overcrowding the pot, add the shrimp and fry for 2 minutes, or until golden brown. Transfer to paper towels to drain, then place in a serving bowl.

5. In a separate bowl, whisk together the mayonnaise, honey, and cream until smooth. Pour over the fried shrimp, then add the walnuts and toss to coat evenly. Serve.

SWAP IT: Swap store-bought candied nuts with homemade. Boil ½ cup of water and ½ cup of sugar in a small pot until it thickens into a syrup. Add the walnuts and stir until the syrup turns golden brown, about 5 minutes. Pour them onto a baking sheet to cool.

Wasabi Soy Salmon

NUT-FREE ❁ FASTER THAN DELIVERY

Americans were introduced to wasabi when sushi was brought over by the Japanese, but 99 percent of what we know as wasabi is fake, made with horseradish, food coloring, and some chemicals. The real wasabi root is delicate, slightly sweet, and doesn't sting as much, but it's too expensive to be commonly served.

SERVES 4
PREP TIME: 5 minutes
COOK TIME: 8 minutes

1 pound salmon, patted dry and cut into 1-inch-thick slices

1 teaspoon salt

½ teaspoon freshly ground black pepper

1 tablespoon sake

3 tablespoons canola oil, divided

½ teaspoon wasabi

¼ cup soy sauce

3 tablespoons honey

2 tablespoons toasted sesame oil

1. Place the salmon in a bowl and add the salt, pepper, sake, and 1 tablespoon of canola oil, mixing to coat evenly.

2. In a large sauté pan or skillet, pour in the remaining 2 tablespoons of canola oil and heat on high. Add the salmon and sear on all sides for 1 minute, for a total of 4 minutes. Transfer to a serving plate.

3. In a small bowl, whisk together the wasabi, soy sauce, honey, and sesame oil. Pour the sauce over the salmon and serve.

INGREDIENT TIP: Cook the salmon medium-rare to medium. Use farm-raised Atlantic salmon for a fattier, more tender cut.

Hibachi Garlic Prawns

NUT-FREE ❀ **FASTER THAN DELIVERY**

Benihana opened his first teppanyaki steakhouse in New York In 1964 and since then, it has become the most famous Japanese steakhouse in the United States. Theatrical cooking combined with Western ingredients, such as lobster, scallops, chicken, steak, and salad, got Americans hooked.

SERVES 4
PREP TIME: 15 minutes
COOK TIME: 5 minutes

½ cup unsalted butter, at room temperature

1½ tablespoons lemon juice

1 teaspoon soy sauce

2 garlic cloves, minced

1 teaspoon canola oil

1 pound prawns, shelled and devcined

½ teaspoon salt

½ teaspoon freshly ground black pepper

1. In a medium bowl, fold together the butter, lemon juice, soy sauce, and garlic until fully mixed, about 1 minute. Set aside.

2. In a wok, pour in the oil and heat on high until the oil smokes. Add the prawns and sauté for 2 minutes on each side.

3. Add 4 teaspoons of the garlic butter and cook the prawns for 2 more minutes on each side, or until slightly brown.

4. Season with the salt and pepper and serve.

INGREDIENT TIP: Store leftover garlic butter and use it to make garlic bread or as a topping for fried rice, baked potato, grilled fish, or steaks.

Tuna Poke Bowl

NUT-FREE ❁ FASTER THAN DELIVERY

Poke bowls have been popping up everywhere in the major cities of America. Poke originates from Hawaii. It was originally made with raw diced fish marinated with salt, seaweed, and crushed nuts. But over time, due to the influx of Asian immigrants into Hawaii, traditional poke ingredients were replaced with others such as furikake, wasabi, and fish eggs.

YIELD: Serves 4
PREP TIME: 10 minutes

1 Fuji apple, diced

2 tablespoons toasted sesame oil

Zest and juice of 1 lemon

2 tablespoons soy sauce

2 teaspoons sriracha or ½ teaspoon wasabi

¼ cup chopped scallions

2 tablespoons toasted sesame seeds

1 pound high-quality ahi tuna or maguro, diced

1. In a large bowl, whisk together the apple, sesame oil, lemon zest and juice, soy sauce, sriracha, scallions, and sesame seeds until smooth.

2. Add the tuna, then mix and serve.

SWAP IT: Swap the apple for an avocado and add mayonnaise for a creamier poke. Or swap scallions for red onions. The beauty of poke is that you can play with different ingredients.

Sugarcane Shrimp

GLUTEN-FREE ❀ NUT-FREE ❀ SOY-FREE ❀ FASTER THAN DELIVERY

Over time, Americans have become more adventurous with food and want to taste new flavors and textures. There is a greater demand for more exotic ingredients, making dishes such as sugarcane shrimp possible in the United States. This crisp, moist, fried shrimp meatball dipped in spicy, sweet sauce is divine.

SERVES 4
PREP TIME: 10 minutes, plus 3 hours to chill
COOK TIME: 10 minutes

3 pieces sugarcane

¾ pound medium shrimp, peeled and deveined

½ teaspoon toasted sesame oil

1 egg white

1 teaspoon salt

½ teaspoon sugar

1½ cups canola oil

¼ cup sriracha

¼ cup honey

1. Peel the sugarcane and cut it into 4 pieces (about 3 inches long) to make 12 pieces. Set aside.

2. In a blender, combine the shrimp, sesame oil, egg white, salt, and sugar and pulse until smooth.

3. Transfer the shrimp mixture into a bowl, then cover with plastic wrap and chill for 3 hours.

4. Using your hands, form the shrimp mixture into an elongated round ball, something that resembles almost a leaner football. Wrap the shrimp mixture patty around the sugarcane.

5. In a Dutch oven, pour in the canola oil and heat to 350°F. Use a deep-fry thermometer to check the temperature.

6. Working in two batches, add the elongated round shrimp balls and fry for 2 minutes on each side, until golden brown.

7. Whisk together the sriracha and honey. Serve with the shrimp balls as a dipping sauce.

SWAP IT: If sugarcane can't be found, cook without it, then garnish the dish with minced pineapple on top to add a fruity sweetness.

Fish in Caramel Sauce (Ca Kho To)

NUT-FREE ❀ FASTER THAN DELIVERY

Ca kho to is a braised and caramelized fish served alongside rice that's commonly made at home using beef, pork, and chicken. The sauce in this local dish transported to the United States and has garnered attention from American chefs. It's essentially sweetened fish sauce that is thick and smooth like caramel. Now you can make it at home.

SERVES 4
PREP TIME: 5 minutes
COOK TIME: 35 minutes

3 tablespoons sugar

2 tablespoons canola oil

6 catfish fillets, halved

3 garlic cloves, minced

3 shallots, minced

2 tablespoons fish sauce

1 cup coconut water

1. In a Dutch oven, put in the sugar and heat on medium, whisking until the sugar melts and turns light brown, about 2 minutes. Immediately add the oil and whisk to cool down the caramel.

2. Add the fish and cook on each side for 1 minute. Add the garlic, shallots, fish sauce, and coconut water, reduce the heat to low, and simmer for 6 minutes, or until the fish is cooked through. Serve.

SWAP IT: For a spicier kick, add ginger and chopped fresh Thai chiles. Swap catfish for tilapia or sea bass.

Coconut Clams with Lime

NUT-FREE ✿ FASTER THAN DELIVERY

This dish is a take on steamed clams (*moules-frites*), where fresh shellfish simmers in a tasty broth and is served with crusty grilled bread. Rather than simmering in garlic, white wine, parsley, and butter, this version is inspired by Thai flavors: chile, cilantro, fish sauce, and coconut milk. Southeast Asian–inspired clam steamers are now appearing at Western bistros and gastropubs.

SERVES 4
PREP TIME: 10 minutes
COOK TIME: 5 minutes

1 tablespoon canola oil

4 garlic cloves, sliced

3 Thai chiles

1 (13.5-ounce) can full-fat coconut milk

2 tablespoons soy sauce

1 tablespoon fish sauce

1 teaspoon sugar

3 pounds fresh clams, rinsed and scrubbed

½ cup minced fresh cilantro

Juice of 2 limes and zest

1. In a wok, pour in the oil and heat on high. Add the garlic and chiles and stir-fry for 30 seconds.

2. Add the coconut milk, soy sauce, fish sauce, and sugar and bring to a boil.

3. Add the clams, cover, and bring to a boil. Cook for 4 minutes, or until the clam shells open.

4. Remove from the heat. Add the cilantro and lime juice and zest and stir. Serve.

SWAP IT: Swap clams for mussels and serve with crusty grilled bread to sop up the beautiful broth.

Fried Tilapia with Salsa

GLUTEN-FREE ❀ NUT-FREE ❀ SOY-FREE ❀ FASTER THAN DELIVERY

This is a take on a traditional Filipino dish that involves frying a whole tilapia with the head and tail and serving it with salsa. Here, a whole fish is swapped with a fillet. Filipino food is hugely influenced by colonizers of Chinese, Malay, Arab, and Spanish descent, which explains why salsa can be found in their cuisine.

SERVES 4
PREP TIME: 10 minutes
COOK TIME: 8 minutes

2 garlic cloves, minced

1 beefsteak tomato, diced

¼ cup chopped
    fresh cilantro

Juice of 1 lime

3 tablespoons extra-virgin
    olive oil

2 teaspoons salt, divided

4 tilapia fillets, sliced down
    the middle to create
    8 fillets

2 eggs, whisked

½ cup cornstarch

1½ cups canola oil

1. In a bowl, combine the garlic, tomato, cilantro, lime juice, olive oil, and 1 teaspoon of salt. Set aside.

2. Place the fish in a large bowl and add the eggs, mixing to coat.

3. Place the cornstarch in a shallow bowl. Dredge each piece of fish until well-coated.

4. In a Dutch oven, pour in the canola oil and heat on high to 350°F. Use a deep-fry thermometer to check the temperature.

5. Working in batches to avoid overcrowding the pot, add the fish and fry on each side for 4 minutes, or until golden brown. Transfer to paper towels to drain. Season with the remaining 1 teaspoon of salt while hot.

6. Serve the fish on a plate and spoon salsa over it.

> **SWAP IT:** For the salsa, add mangos and sugar for a tropical twist. If fresh tilapia can't be found, use frozen and defrost before frying.

MATCHA LADYFINGER PARFAIT, PAGE 145

NINE
Dessert

Fried Banana with Ice Cream 143

Mango Sticky Rice 144

Matcha Ladyfinger Parfait 145

Pineapple Yakult Ice Pops 146

Peanut Butter Milk Toast 147

Pumpkin Rice Cake 148

Steamed Cupcake 149

Filipino Chocolate Rice Pudding (Champorado) 150

Grass Jelly Almond Ice-Cream Float 151

Honeydew Sago 152

In Asian cuisine, dessert is often enjoyed in between meals as a snack instead of a last course. Desserts also serve a purpose. In hotter Southeast Asian climates, desserts are largely liquid-based, made with beans, herbs, and fruit—a combination that helps cool down the body from heat and replenish fluids. In northern regions of Asia, desserts are served hot, steamed, fried, or boiled into soups to keep the body warm and the blood flowing. In the United States, dessert completes a meal and pleases the taste buds. This explains why the ingredients used to make desserts vary greatly between Asia and the West. Asians rely heavily on healthy ingredients such as glutinous rice, tapioca, beans, fruit, and coconut milk. Many of the recipes in this chapter are gluten-free and egg-free, perfect for plant-based diets.

FUN ASIAN FOOD FACT

Ice cream is thought to have been invented by the Chinese back in 200 BCE. The Chinese King Tang of Shang had his men mix ice with milk and freeze it by packing it in snow, creating the first version of ice cream. The Chinese are also believed to have created the first ice-cream machine. They filled pots with a syrupy concoction, which was then packed in vessels filled with snow and salt. When Marco Polo learned about this delightful creation, he brought it from China to Italy, where they put their own spin on it: gelato. Even though ice cream was invented in China, Chinese cuisine is not known for its ice cream. In the last few years, Asian flavors such as lychee, matcha, Thai tea, and coconut are becoming popular. Try our Pumpkin Rice Cake (page 148) with vanilla ice cream and cinnamon powder or a scoop of chocolate ice cream over Peanut Butter Milk Toast (page 147).

Fried Banana with Ice Cream

GLUTEN-FREE ❁ NUT-FREE ❁ SOY-FREE ❁ VEGETARIAN
FASTER THAN DELIVERY

Fried banana is a popular dessert and street food snack in Thailand and in other Southeast Asian countries. A light, airy, crispy batter wrapped around the soft, sweet, custard-like banana tastes incredible with a spoonful of cold ice cream. This dessert was an easy import into the United States, as banana is a household staple.

SERVES 4
PREP TIME: 10 minutes
COOK TIME: 8 minutes

4 soft ripe bananas

1 egg

¼ teaspoon baking soda

½ cup water

½ cup cornstarch

2 tablespoons sugar

¼ cup dried shredded coconut

2 cups canola oil or peanut oil

¼ cup rice flour

1 pint coconut ice cream

1. Peel the bananas and cut crosswise into 3 equal sections, then halve each piece lengthwise.

2. In a medium bowl, whisk together the egg, baking soda, water, cornstarch, sugar, and coconut until a smooth batter forms.

3. In a Dutch oven, pour in the oil and heat on high to 350°F. Use a deep-fry thermometer to check the temperature.

4. Place the rice flour in a shallow bowl. Coat each banana piece in the flour, then dredge them in the batter.

5. Working in batches to avoid overcrowding the pot, add the banana and fry until golden brown, about 2 minutes. Transfer to paper towels to drain.

6. Serve warm with a side of coconut ice cream.

SWAP IT: Swap coconut ice cream for vanilla or chocolate.

Mango Sticky Rice

GLUTEN-FREE ❀ NUT-FREE ❀ VEGETARIAN ❀ 5 INGREDIENTS TAKEOUT FAVORITE

This is probably the most iconic Thai dessert. What's not to love about this dish? Just think of it as a stickier version of rice pudding served with sweet, tart mangos. It's available for delivery at many Thai restaurants but is best when fresh made, straight off the stove.

SERVES 4
PREP TIME: 30 minutes
COOK TIME: 45 minutes

1 cup glutinous rice

1½ cups water, divided

1 (13-ounce) can full-fat coconut milk, divided

4 tablespoons sugar, divided

¼ teaspoon salt

2 ripe mangos, peeled and sliced thin

1. In a saucepot, soak the rice in 1 cup of water for 30 minutes.

2. Place the pot over high heat. Add the remaining ½ cup of water, half the coconut milk, 1 tablespoon of sugar, and the salt and bring to a boil. Stir twice, reduce the heat to low, and cover, leaving a small opening where steam can escape. Cook for 30 minutes.

3. Remove from the heat, cover fully, and set aside to steam for 10 minutes.

4. In a separate saucepan over medium heat, combine the remaining half of the coconut milk and 3 tablespoons of sugar and cook for 5 minutes.

5. Place a scoop of coconut rice in a shallow bowl, drape 4 to 6 slices of mango over the rice, and drizzle the coconut sauce on top. Serve.

INGREDIENT TIP: Fresh mangos and glutinous rice can be found at Asian markets. If mangos are not in season, use thawed frozen mango.

Matcha Ladyfinger Parfait

NUT-FREE ❁ SOY-FREE ❁ VEGETARIAN ❁ FASTER THAN DELIVERY

Japanese matcha is traditionally enjoyed at tea ceremonies where the preparation, serving, and drinking of the green tea becomes a form of meditative enjoyment. Matcha drinks have become quite the rage in the United States. Many specialty coffee shops now offer matcha lattes. This grassy, herbaceous powder works great in desserts.

SERVES 4
PREP TIME: 15 minutes

1½ cups strawberries, diced, plus more for garnish

7 tablespoons sugar, divided

2 teaspoons matcha powder

2 cups heavy (whipping) cream

2 teaspoons vanilla extract

12 ladyfingers, crumbled, plus more for garnish

1. In a small bowl, marinate the strawberries with 3 tablespoons of sugar. Set aside while you make the whipped cream.

2. Combine the matcha, cream, vanilla, and remaining 4 tablespoons of sugar in a blender. Pulse for 20 seconds, or until the liquid becomes a firm whipped cream. To test, turn the blender upside down. If the cream stays put, it's done.

3. Use small bowls or glasses to assemble. Layer the ladyfingers on the bottom. Top with the strawberries, then cover with matcha whipped cream. Garnish with more ladyfingers and strawberries and serve.

SWAP IT: Canned peaches are great if strawberries are not in season. If ladyfingers can't be found, use Nilla Wafers dipped in heavy (whipping) cream before layering.

Pineapple Yakult Ice Pops

GLUTEN-FREE ✿ NUT-FREE ✿ SOY-FREE ✿ VEGETARIAN ✿ 5 INGREDIENTS

Yakult is a sweetened and slightly tart fermented probiotic beverage with *Lactobacillus,* the same bacteria found in yogurt, invented in Japan in 1930. This mini, one-size beverage has a distinctive red foil seal that is easily recognizable and is widely popular in Asia. It was introduced to the United States in 1999. Now you can buy it at Costco, Asian markets, and online.

SERVES 4
PREP TIME: 10 minutes, plus overnight to freeze

4 bottles Yakult

1 (20-ounce) can pineapple chunks

1. In a blender, combine the Yakult and half of the pineapple and pulse to combine.

2. Fill 4 to 6 ice pop molds halfway with the Yakult mixture. Add the pineapple chunks and then more Yakult until the molds are filled.

3. Freeze overnight, then serve.

> **SERVING TIP:** If you don't own ice pop molds, use disposable paper cups or clean yogurt cups. Place a wooden stick in after the liquid has been poured in, and then freeze.

Peanut Butter Milk Toast

SOY-FREE & VEGETARIAN & 5 INGREDIENTS & FASTER THAN DELIVERY

Toast with condensed milk (*cha chaan teng*) is a common Item al Ilong Kong cafés. It's usually enjoyed with milk tea as an afternoon snack. Here in the United States, where the dish has taken on a life of its own, Hong Kong–style dessert cafés serve this type of toast with different toppings, such as ice cream, fruit, chocolate sauce, or whipped cream.

SERVES 4
PREP TIME: 10 minutes
COOK TIME: 5 minutes

8 tablespoons
  peanut butter

4 slices thick-cut
  milk bread

8 tablespoons
  condensed milk

1. Spread 2 tablespoons of peanut butter on each slice of bread.

2. Toast the bread in the oven for medium doneness, about 4 minutes.

3. Remove the toast, plate it, and drizzle each slice with 2 tablespoons of condensed milk. Serve.

SWAP IT: If Japanese-style milk bread can't be found, use Texas toast. The key is using thick slices of bread.

Pumpkin Rice Cake

**GLUTEN-FREE ❀ SOY-FREE ❀ VEGETARIAN ❀ 5 INGREDIENTS
FASTER THAN DELIVERY**

This is a take on a traditional Chinese dessert, which is made with kabocha squash, a Japanese pumpkin. These soft, sticky, chewy pancakes coated in sesame seeds are eaten warm and enjoyed during celebratory events. Here, we use Western pumpkin and swap out the sesame seeds for powdered sugar. It's a great gluten-free alternative to pancakes, and with powdered sugar and a dollop of ice cream, it makes for a great dessert.

SERVES 4
PREP TIME: 10 minutes
COOK TIME: 8 minutes

7 ounces canned pumpkin puree

2 cups glutinous rice flour

2 ½ teaspoons granulated sugar

¼ cup peanut oil, divided

¼ cup powdered sugar

1. In a medium bowl, using a fork, mix together the pumpkin, flour, granulated sugar, and 3 tablespoons of oil. Once incorporated, use your hands to knead the mixture into a smooth dough.

2. Form the dough into golf ball–size balls. With the palms of your hands, press each ball into a ½-inch-thick disk.

3. In a large nonstick sauté pan, pour in the remaining 1 tablespoon of oil and heat on high. Add the disks, then reduce the heat to medium and pan-fry for 2 minutes on each side, or until golden brown.

4. Transfer the pancakes to serving plates. Using a sieve, dust the powdered sugar on top and serve.

INGREDIENT TIP: Glutinous rice flour can be found in Asian markets and online. It adds a sticky and chewy consistency to pancakes and is a common flour used in Asian desserts.

Steamed Cupcake

NUT-FREE ✿ SOY-FREE ✿ VEGETARIAN ✿ 5 INGREDIENTS
FASTER THAN DELIVERY

Baking desserts in an oven is not a cooking technique used in Asian cuisines, which explains why many of their desserts are steamed, boiled, or fried. Steamed cupcakes may sound difficult to master, but it's actually one of the easiest desserts you can make. It's light, fluffy, and moist, but also slightly chewy. It's a great alternative to the denser-style American cupcakes.

MAKES 16 cupcakes
PREP TIME: 5 minutes
COOK TIME: 20 minutes

1 box yellow cake mix, such as Betty Crocker

1 cup glutinous rice flour

2 tablespoons toasted sesame seeds

1. Line 16 individual cupcake tins with liners.

2. Follow the instructions on the cake mix box, but mix for only 1 minute. Then add the glutinous flour and mix for 1 minute. Do not overmix.

3. Using an ice-cream scoop, fill each prepared tin about halfway (do not fill to the top). Sprinkle sesame seeds on top.

4. Fill a pot halfway with water and bring to a boil over high heat. Working in two batches, arrange the cupcakes on a steaming rack, place in the pot, cover, and steam for 20 minutes. Serve warm.

SERVING TIP: Unlike cupcakes baked in the oven where the top is smooth and round, steamed cupcakes with glutinous flour will produce a top that blossoms like a flower. To play into the flower cupcake look, use food coloring to make different colored cupcakes.

Filipino Chocolate Rice Pudding (Champorado)

GLUTEN-FREE ❁ **NUT-FREE** ❁ **SOY-FREE** ❁ **VEGETARIAN** ❁ **5 INGREDIENTS**
FASTER THAN DELIVERY

During the Galleon Trade, Mexican traders introduced the Philippines to a Mexican hot chocolate called *champurrado*. Filipinos adopted this drink and added the rice component to make a new dish. In the Philippines, this dish is eaten as breakfast and sometimes as a snack. But here in the United States, it's been introduced as a delicious dessert.

SERVES 4
PREP TIME: 5 minutes
COOK TIME: 25 minutes

2 cups glutinous rice

4½ cups water

1 cup cocoa powder

1 cup sugar

1 cup evaporated milk

1. Rinse the rice under water, then place in a large nonstick saucepan and heat on high.

2. Add the water and bring to a boil. Then immediately reduce the heat to low and cook for 20 minutes, stirring occasionally.

3. Add the cocoa powder and sugar and whisk for 2 minutes, or until fully dissolved and incorporated.

4. Remove from the heat and let it sit for 40 minutes, or until it's cooled enough to eat.

5. Serve in small bowls and top with the evaporated milk.

SERVING TIP: The pudding can be refrigerated for 3 days and enjoyed cold or reheated.

Grass Jelly Almond Ice-Cream Float

GLUTEN-FREE ❀ SOY-FREE ❀ VEGETARIAN ❀ 5 INGREDIENTS FASTER THAN DELIVERY

This refreshing drink is enjoyed as a snack, a dessert, and sometimes even as a complement to a main dish. Grass jelly has a cooling, minty, herbal taste, which complements creamy and sweet combinations. It's become a common topping for boba drinks in the United States. This version is a play on an ice-cream float. The addition of ice cream makes it more American but also adds decadence.

SERVES 4
PREP TIME: 10 minutes

1 (24-ounce) can grass jelly, cubed

4 cups vanilla almond milk

4 scoops of vanilla ice cream

1. Divide the grass jelly among 4 tall glasses, filling only halfway.

2. Pour the almond milk into each glass until three-fourths full.

3. Top with a scoop of ice cream. Enjoy with a straw and long spoon.

SERVING TIP: This dessert is to be enjoyed with a spoon, so you can taste the jelly along with the ice cream and milk. Once the ice cream melts down a bit, sip with a straw to finish off the dessert.

Honeydew Sago

**GLUTEN-FREE ❁ SOY-FREE ❁ VEGETARIAN ❁ 5 INGREDIENTS
FASTER THAN DELIVERY**

Sago desserts are common in Southeast Asia. These slightly chewy but soft, smooth pearls have made their way into America's tummies through delicious Asian American desserts and drinks as well as through Europe and Brazil, where they're used in puddings.

**SERVES 4
PREP TIME:** 5 minutes
COOK TIME: 30 minutes

4 cups water

½ cup small dry sago

1 cup full-fat coconut milk

½ can evaporated milk

1 small honeydew melon

1 cup condensed milk

1. In a saucepot, bring the water to a boil over high heat. Then reduce the heat to medium, add the sago, and bring to a simmer. Stir, cover, and simmer for 20 minutes, stirring occasionally to prevent the sago from sticking to the bottom.

2. Remove from the heat, stir again, then cover and set aside for 15 minutes, until the sago is translucent.

3. Strain the sago in a sieve and rinse with cold water to wash off residual starch. Divide the sago into small bowls.

4. In a medium bowl, whisk together the coconut milk and evaporated milk. Pour over the sago, filling the bowls three-quarters full.

5. With a melon baller, scoop 4 to 6 balls of honeydew into each bowl. Drizzle the condensed milk on top and serve.

INGREDIENT TIP: Find sago at your local Asian market or buy it online. Depending on which sago you purchase, following instructions on the bag for cooking is advisable. The instructions above are only for small-size sago.

MENUS

❀

Spicy Chinese

SERVES 4 ❀ **PREP TIME:** 40 minutes ❀ **COOK TIME:** 1 hour

This menu is an ode to the cuisine of Northern China, specifically from the Sichuan region. Cook up spicy mapo tofu and pan-sear some beautiful dumplings. These restaurant-quality dishes will wow any guests you entertain at home.

CHICKEN POT STICKERS (GUŌTIĒ), page 26
MAPO TOFU WITH PORK, page 120
GARLIC BOK CHOY, page 82
STEAMED RICE, page 19

Sunday Supper Filipino Style

SERVES 4 ❀ **PREP TIME:** 30 minutes, plus overnight for dessert ❀ **COOK TIME:** 1 hour

Finding new dishes to throw into your Sunday supper rotation can be challenging at times. But this Filipino-inspired menu is not only easy to master but also incredibly delicious. Crispy spring rolls paired with savory, tender stewed chicken over rice, followed by a decadent chocolate-based dessert sounds like a meal you would get at a restaurant and not at home. To save time in the kitchen, prepare the dessert the night before and chill. Wrap lumpias with your family while the chicken adobo and rice are cooking. That way, everything can come out hot and fresh at the same time.

LUMPIA, page 30
CHICKEN ADOBO, page 108
STEAMED RICE, page 19
**FILIPINO CHOCOLATE RICE PUDDING
(CHAMPORADO),** page 150

Vietnamese Brunch

SERVES 4 ❀ PREP TIME: 1 hour ❀ COOK TIME: 30 minutes

Put a Southeast Asian twist on brunch with friends. Rather than the usual eggs, bacon, toast, and pancake offerings, try serving a unique brunch with eggs, vermicelli salad, and grass jelly. You've got something with eggs, something savory, and something sweet.

RICE NOODLES WITH SHRIMP (BÚN CHẢ), page 44
GREEN BEAN OMELET, page 91
GRASS JELLY ALMOND ICE-CREAM FLOAT, page 151

Korean Barbecue Night

SERVES 4 ❀ PREP TIME: 30 minutes, plus overnight to marinate
COOK TIME: 40 minutes

This menu is great for an outdoor barbecue. To save time in the kitchen the day of the party, prepare the bean sprouts earlier in the day and store in the refrigerator to serve cold, marinate the short ribs the night before, and cook the japchae right before serving. You'll be the star of the party!

SESAME BEAN SPROUTS, page 88
SWEET AND SPICY KOREAN SHORT RIBS (GALBI), page 125
JAPCHAE, page 51

Japanese Happy Hour

SERVES 4 ❀ PREP TIME: 1 hour ❀ COOK TIME: 40 minutes

The beauty of this menu is that it can be served buffet-style for a large group of friends. Prepare a large pot of ramen broth, then place toppings on the side so guests can build their own ramen bowls. Even the chicken karaage can be added as a topping to the ramen bowls. Serve edamame as a bar bite when guests arrive, alongside some nuts.

SALT AND PEPPER EDAMAME, page 81
CHICKEN KARAAGE, page 106
SHOYU PORK CORN RAMEN, page 49

Thai Date Night

SERVES: 4 ✿ PREP TIME: 20 minutes ✿ COOK TIME: 45 minutes

To keep things streamlined on your Thai-inspired date night, prepare the soup ahead of time. Reheat it while you cook the drunken noodles, so both can be served at the same time. Once dinner is done, fry the bananas, as this dessert is best enjoyed hot.

THAI COCONUT SOUP (TOM KHA GAI), page 67
DRUNKEN NOODLES WITH CHICKEN (PAD KEE MAO), page 46
FRIED BANANA WITH ICE CREAM, page 143

Pan-Asian Dinner

SERVES 4 ✿ PREP TIME: 30 minutes ✿ COOK TIME: 1 hour 15 minutes

This flavorful menu is salty, savory, sweet, sticky, crispy, and creamy. Dinner is sure to excite your taste buds. Prepare the coconut rice and Cambodian pork first and let them simmer while you work on the crab rangoon. After wrapping and frying the rangoon, your rice and pork should be close to done.

CRAB RANGOON, page 34
CAMBODIAN PORK CURRY, page 71
COCONUT STICKY RICE, page 47

Vegetarian Feast

SERVES 4 ✿ PREP TIME: 30 minutes ✿ COOK TIME: 30 minutes

This vegetarian feast is delicious hot or cold. Prepare extras so you can have leftovers. Pack up in bento boxes and enjoy cold for lunch at work. These flavors absorb beautifully when left overnight and are just as tasty when eaten the next day.

GREEN PAPAYA SALAD (SOM TUM), page 93
CRISPY TOFU WITH PEANUT SAUCE, page 95
DRY-BRAISED GREEN BEANS WITH MUSHROOMS, page 85

MEASUREMENT CONVERSIONS

VOLUME EQUIVALENTS (LIQUID)

US STANDARD	US STANDARD (OUNCES)	METRIC (APPROX.)
2 tablespoons	1 fl. oz.	30 mL
¼ cup	2 fl. oz.	60 mL
½ cup	4 fl. oz.	120 mL
1 cup	8 fl. oz.	240 mL
1½ cups	12 fl. oz.	355 mL
2 cups or 1 pint	16 fl. oz.	475 mL
4 cups or 1 quart	32 fl. oz.	1 L
1 gallon	128 fl. oz.	4 L

OVEN TEMPERATURES

FAHRENHEIT (F)	CELSIUS (C) (APPROX.)
250°	120°
300°	150°
325°	165°
350°	180°
375°	190°
400°	200°
425°	220°
450°	230°

VOLUME EQUIVALENTS (DRY)

US STANDARD	METRIC (APPROX.)
⅛ teaspoon	0.5 mL
¼ teaspoon	1 mL
½ teaspoon	2 mL
¾ teaspoon	4 mL
1 teaspoon	5 mL
1 tablespoon	15 mL
¼ cup	59 mL
⅓ cup	79 mL
½ cup	118 mL
⅔ cup	156 mL
¾ cup	177 mL
1 cup	235 mL
2 cups or 1 pint	475 mL
3 cups	700 mL
4 cups or 1 quart	1 L

WEIGHT EQUIVALENTS

US STANDARD	METRIC (APPROX.)
½ ounce	15 g
1 ounce	30 g
2 ounces	60 g
4 ounces	115 g
8 ounces	225 g
12 ounces	340 g
16 ounces or 1 pound	455 g

RESOURCES

Brown, Tanner. "China's Pork Crisis Is Bigger Than You Think." MarketWatch. November 16, 2019. MarketWatch.com/story/chinas -pork-crisis-is-bigger-than-you-think-2019-11-11.

Budiman, Abby, Anthony Cilluffo, and Neil G Ruiz. "Key Facts about Asian Origin Groups in the US." Pew Research Center. May 22, 2019. PewResearch.org/fact-tank/2019/05/22/key-facts-about-asian -origin-groups-in-the-u-s.

Chang, K. C. "Food in Chinese Culture." *Asia Blog*. Asia Society, September 2, 2008. AsiaSociety.org/blog/asia/food-chinese-culture.

Cruz, Heidi. "Gyudon: Beef Bowl." *All in Japan* (Blog). January 6, 2013. AllInJapan.org/gyudon-beef-bowl.

Davison, Gary Marvin, and Barbara E. Reed. *Culture and Customs of Taiwan*. Westport, Connecticut: Greenwood Publishing Group, 1998.

Jiahui, Sun. "The Making of Mapo Tofu." *China Daily*. Last Modified September 6, 2015. chinadaily.com.cn/kindle/2015-09/06/content_ 21798522.htm.

Jones, Nicholas A. *The Asian Population in the United States: Results from the 2010 Census*. US Census Bureau. May 2, 2012. SSA.gov/people/aapi /materials/pdfs/2010census-data.pdf.

Lee, Hang-Shuen. "Healthy Eating in Traditional Chinese Medicine." DW Akademie. January 18, 2019. DW.com/en/healthy-eating-in -traditional-chinese-medicine/a-18619239.

Lewis, Danny. "British Monks Discovered a Curry Recipe in a 200-Year Old Cookbook." *Smithsonian Magazine.* February 5, 2016. SmithsonianMag.com/smart-news/british-monks-discovered-curry-recipe-200-year-old-cookbook-180957979.

Ma, Guansheng. "Food, Eating Behavior, and Culture in Chinese Society." *Journal of Ethnic Foods* 2, no. 4 (December 2015): 195–99, DOI.org/10.1016/j.jef.2015.11.004.

Nelson, Angela. "5 Things You Never Knew about Wasabi." Mother Nature Network. September 26, 2016. MNN.com/food/healthy-eating/stories/things-you-never-knew-about-wasabi.

Papademetriou, M.K. "Rice Production in The Asia-Pacific Region: Issues and Perspectives." Food and Agriculture Organization of the United Nations. Accessed February 25, 2020. FAO.org/3/x6905e/x6905e04.htm.

Pew Research Center. "Thai in the US Fact Sheet." September 8, 2017. PewSocialTrends.org/fact-sheet/asian-americans-thai-in-the-u-s.

Pew Research Center. "Top US Metropolitan Areas by Korean Population." September 8, 2017. PewSocialTrends.org/chart/top-10-u-s-metropolitan-areas-by-korean-population.

Proximity One. "America's Asian Population Demographic Patterns and Trends." Accessed February 25, 2020. ProximityOne.com/asian_demographics.htm.

Roman, Brent, and Susan Russell. "Southeast Asian Food and Culture." Lesson plan, Northern Illinois University, Dekalb, Illinois, November 16, 2009. NIU.edu/cseas/_pdf/lesson-plans/k-12/southeast-asian-food-culture.pdf.

Shurtleff, William, and Akiki Aoyagi. "History of Tofu." SoyInfo Center. Accessed February 25, 2020. SoyInfoCenter.com/HSS/tofu1.php.

Sul, Sean. "Delicious Roots: The Story of Budae Jjigae." Kimchee Guest-house. December 1, 2016. KimcheeGuestHouse.com/delicious-roots-story-budae-jjigae.

Wertz, Richard R. "Regional Cuisine." Cultural Heritage of China. Accessed February 25, 2020. iBiblio.org/chineseculture/contents/food/p-food-c01s03.html.

World Population Review. "Honolulu, Hawaii Population 2020." Accessed February 25, 2020. WorldPopulationReview.com/us-cities/honolulu-population.

Zong, Jie, and Jeanne Batalova. "Filipino Immigrants in the United States." Migration Policy Institute. March 14, 2018. MigrationPolicy.org/article/filipino-immigrants-united-states.

INDEX

COUNTRY OF ORIGIN INDEX

ACKNOWLEDGMENTS

❀

I want to thank the following people who made it possible for me to write this book.

My father, Peter Fang, who has guided me, supported me, and taught me to become the chef and businesswoman that I am today. I wouldn't be where I am today if it weren't for my biggest role model.

My mother, Lily Fang, for showing me what hard work and devotion mean when it comes to being a mother, wife, and business partner. She's an inspiration.

My husband, Caleb Sima, for always pushing me to do more and never settling for less. For supporting me in every way possible when I needed it the most, whether at work or at home.

My PR Team at Glodow Nead—Sonia, Carly, John, and Jeff—for helping me grow as a chef and brand, opening doors that have allowed me to share my voice, my passion, and food through various media outlets, from print to television and radio.

Tamara Palmer and Kathy Leong, for encouraging me to pursue writing.

Callisto Media, especially Arturo and Wesley, for giving me the incredible opportunity to do something I've always wanted to do: write a cookbook.

And, to my two babies, Ava and Neo. I hope this book will make you two proud and, if anything, inspire you two to cook and learn the importance food plays in our lives.

ABOUT THE AUTHOR

Kathy Fang is a San Francisco native who grew up in the kitchen of her family's restaurant, House of Nanking. She grew into adulthood as the co-owner and chef of Fang Restaurant with her father in 2009. Kathy blends her family's Cantonese and Shanghainese heritage with a cooking style that inspires her to create sophisticated and multicultural cuisine. Now a rising star in the cooking world, Kathy teaches students to create easy and delicious dishes and has competed on different Food Network shows, including *Cutthroat Kitchen*, *Guy's Grocery Games*, and *Chopped*, where she is a two-time champion.